Praise for Climb

"As a climber and sport psychologist, Rebecca Williams' book, "Climb Smarter", explores her practical approach to mental challenges in a way that is easy to understand. I feel mentally stronger after reading and I can't wait to go climbing again."

~ Madeline Crane: Climbing Psychology

"In Climb Smarter, Dr Williams has given the climbing community a mental training guide that has everything in one text: Scientific rigor, the depth of knowledge, compassion and understanding that comes from a clinical psychologist, and the hands-on experience of a seasoned climbing coach. This text is set to become the industry benchmark by which all mental training advice can be measured. Whether your inner struggles are with confidence, motivation, falling or failing, all the tools you need to grow as a climber and a human can be found in this comprehensive guide. To really excel at climbing, training the mind needs to become a routine behaviour - and for that journey I cannot recommend this book highly enough."

~ John Kettle: Climbing Coach Performance Coach, WMCI

"An extraordinary and brilliant book, with golden insightful nuggets from the first chapter all the way through. These nuggets will help improve your climbing and quite possibly your lifestyle, taking a holistic look at the many factors which can affect our mental state, how to measure them and make changes if we feel we need to. Rebecca brings the science and evidence together in a logical way which is easy to digest. A must buy for any keen climbers wanting to get on top of their head game."

~ James McHaffie: Pro Climber

"Finding your 'why' - in my decades of climbing and coaching I find myself always going back to this fundamental assessment. Regardless if i was considering a scary climb, or when trying to help a frustrated athlete, "what is it that you love about climbing?" is often the central question to ask.

Rebecca Williams' new Climb Smarter Book is of great help for any climbing related inner struggle you might have (or want to help somebody with). It is clearly written and structured and offers actionable exercises as well as case examples that help you to learn about yourself and face climbing's mental challenges.

From life values to climbing values and back - the Climb Smarter Book is a valuable read for everyone - not only climbers!"

~ Udo Neumann: Climbing Coach, Writer

"Climb Smarter is more than a sport psychology book. It is written by a climber for climbers with brilliantly specific explanations, case studies, activities and worksheets to help your mind help your body to take your climbing to the next level."

~ Dr Josephine Perry: Chartered Sport Psychologist, www.performanceinmind.co.uk

CLIMB
SMARTER

CLIMB SMARTER

MENTAL SKILLS AND TECHNIQUES FOR CLIMBING

Dr Rebecca Williams

SEQUOIA
BOOKS

First published in 2022 by Sequoia Books

ISBN
Print: 9781914110146
EPUB: 9781914110153

A CIP record for this book is available from the British Library

Library of Congress Cataloguing-In-Publication Data
Name: Dr Rebecca Williams
Title: Climb Smarter / Dr Rebecca Williams
Description: 1st Edition, Sequoia Books UK 2022
Subjects: LCSH:. Sport Psychology. Sports-Psychological Aspects
Print: 9781914110146
EPUB: 9781914110153

Library of Congress Control Number: 2022903330

Print and Electronic production managed by Deanta Global

Cover Image photographer: Ray Wood
Climber: Alexandra Schweikart on the top pitch of The Mask (E5 6a), Fair Head, Ireland

Contents

Acknowledgements

Three years ago I met a brilliant psychologist working with climbers, at the International Rock Climbing Research Association congress in Chamonix in 2018. We got chatting about shared experiences and ideas, and she encouraged me to write a book about my experiences of coaching climbers. Fast-forward three years and we are continuing to collaborate and develop resources for climbers – thank you Dr Maria Ionel for getting me started on this journey.

Huge thanks also to Pete and Rach Robins for reading some early drafts and giving honest and clear feedback. In the middle (and painful part), I had a lot of help from Pete Edwards; thanks to him for chasing down the elusive references and offering feedback and insights.

Most important of all however, I am extremely grateful to my family – Pete, Tali and Mabon – for supporting me in writing, by (mostly) leaving me alone in the mornings so I could write, and for offering encouragement when I lost motivation. I hope my boys can be inspired to give their own big projects a go in the future (and may they never have to type with a four-year-old on their lap!).

Climber studies

The climber studies are composite case studies of a few of the people I have coached around common themes, over the last 15 years. All names are pseudonyms, and any identifying details have been changed to protect their identities.

Introduction

I first got into sport as a young kid, watching gymnastics on the TV. My parents were both climbers but had given all that up to run a smallholding in North Wales by the time I came along, and they were happy to indulge me in my new-found obsession. A perfectionist child, I excelled at following the training plans, and revelled in learning how to make my body create the twists, turns, jumps and acrobatics I had once watched spellbound on the TV. However, years of training later and after a series of injuries, I had several experiences of what I now know was choking – being completely unable to complete well-rehearsed moves, paralysed with anxiety. Back then, no one mentioned how sport psychology could help, and you were simply seen as either having the head for gym or not. Being unable to overcome my 'episodes' by myself, and with coaches telling me I just didn't have it, in the end I quit the sport, devastated. It left a big hole in my life for some time, before I found other sports to take its place.

Fast-forward 35 years or so, and I've just watched the greatest gymnast of all time, Simone Biles, pull out of an Olympic final due to an attack of the 'twisties'. She was losing track of where she was in space during her double somersaults with triple twists (and who wouldn't?!) and with the full support of her coaches, team and gym community, she prioritised her own welfare over competing. Even more incredible was to see that support translate into coming back into the beam final and winning a medal. I don't know whether she accessed sport psychology help in the interim, but I think it illustrates how the mindset has shifted from 'got it/not got it' to 'let's work on it' for the mental skills required for various sports.

I think the climbing community has been a bit behind the curve in adopting sport psychology techniques. Some still cling to the notion that you either have the head for climbing or you don't, and that fears and worries and mental blocks are 'irrational' and therefore somehow indicate an internal weakness and unsuitability for climbing. This is not something I subscribe to, with both personal and professional experience to the contrary. Over the last 15 years or so, I have watched many coaching clients learn new skills to enhance their climbing, break through personal grade barriers, send their projects or simply enjoy climbing more. Most climbers I know want to improve, and whilst many will opt for physical improvements, fewer will take the arguably harder path of making mental improvements. The gains are less easy to measure, and you have to be diligent in applying yourself over time, but change is possible. No one should write themselves off as not having a head for heights/leading/competing – we can learn how to get our mind and body in sync, with the right tools.

My own climbing journey began quite late as I was studying for my doctorate in clinical psychology. I gave it a try on a National Trust conservation holiday, wherein between hacking at rhododendrons, we had some light relief in the form of climbing. Our instructor was none other than Nick Dixon, and if I had known who he was in climbing circles at the time, I probably would have swooned with stardom! Anyway, a couple of top ropes and I was hooked, taking it up at Rock City climbing wall in Hull as a great stress relief when studying, and meeting a whole new community of people. My progression followed a very similar trajectory as I see in many climbers – rapid progression, plateau and then a huge and catastrophic tail off in performance as I began to realise what the risks were. I was curious as to why my meltdowns happened on easier stuff – next to the bolt on a 5+, stepping over the void on a VDiff, on the easy warm-up routes in Sardinia – and never when I was pushing the boat out. My old demons from gymnastics came back to haunt me, and I floundered around for a while before realising that I had the answers at my finger tips from studying psychology. This time around, I understood what was happening, and by now, sport psychology was a thing and there were research papers, self-help books and advice to be found. I applied the anxiety management techniques I knew from my work as a trainee psychologist, devoured all the papers and self-help books I could find and eventually found a balance in my climbing. I'll never be a mega hard trad leader (E1 was the best I managed), but I realised that for routes I was passionate about, I could manage my nerves and harness the joy I found in unlocking sequences on the rock, and my perfectionistic diligence in finding efficient and flowing movement. These days I mostly boulder, partly due to time (having a young family, a chronic health condition, and being self-employed) but partly also because it's the distillation of what I love about climbing – solving movement puzzles on rock. It's a physical and mental workout, and it reminds me of my days as a gymnast, figuring out how to move my body through space in the most elegant and efficient way possible.

This book brings together all the lessons I learnt as a psychologist and climber, and as a coach to climbers, weaving together the knowledge and covering any gaps in the tapestry with research drawn across from other sports. As soon as I publish this book, I hope it will be quickly updated as climbing research, still in its infancy, will no doubt be given a huge push by the inclusion of climbing in the Olympics. Given its popularity at Tokyo, I suspect funding may follow, and researchers can start finally testing out some of the practices and exercises, and seeing what works, for whom and why. For now, this book represents my best clinical practice-based evidence, outlining common problems climbers have, and how they can be managed to improve their psychological performance and therefore their climbing.

I hope you enjoy learning the broad variety of techniques in this book, applying them to your own climbing, and hopefully finding or re-discovering the inherent joy of moving freely over rock, unencumbered by mental demons. This book is for anyone who ever wished they could improve their headgame for climbing. It covers how to fix common problems climbers face, as well as how to enhance and finesse your performance using mental training strategies. There is also a section on tactics and creative problem-solving, which is a key skill for climbers who feel as though their strategies and movement patterns are stuck in a bit of a rut. It is highly practical, and you won't find any 'just do this' in it; I explain exactly how to develop the skills you need to climb smarter, by using your head, so you can use the physical and technical skills you have to their best ability.

What the book can't do is magically transform your climbing after you read it, unfortunately! Training mental skills is the long game, and you should set yourself a skill, chapter or topic per month to focus on, alongside your regular climbing and training. The aim is to take some of the mystery out of what the key mental attributes for climbing are, help you to understand climbing psychology a little better and give you practical tools to improve your focus, confidence, anxiety and reduce frustrations! Ultimately though, by sorting some of the issues in your climbing, and learning mental skills to enhance how you climb, I hope that you will find more fun and enjoyment in your climbing.

SECTION 1
Planning

This first section is all about planning and preparation – your time and energy are both precious and finite, so make the most of them by spending time at the outset getting all your ducks in a row rather than heading off on a wild goose chase. If you really want to commit to making long-term changes, then some hours spent reflecting, thinking and planning now will pay dividends in terms of being able to direct your efforts to best effect change. If you're not the sort of climber who sets goals, that's ok (plenty of climbers don't and enjoy their climbing just fine), but I'm guessing that you bought this book because you want to improve and have an interest in training your mind to help you climb harder, or climb with less fear and worry.

Being a 'better climber' is a common goal for my coaching clients, and it's a great starting place, but it doesn't tell me or them much about what we need to do for them to improve, or how much better or more relaxed they want to be in order to feel satisfied with their climbing. There is a saying, start with the end in mind, so we need to think about our destination, in order to best plan the best way to get there: what mental skills do we need to develop? Which psychological skills will help us to be a better climber?

We also need to know where we are starting from in the first place, to make sure we don't waste time covering old ground, so a good assessment of our current mental skills is important. We need a reason why to take the improvement journey and inventory of what we need to get from a to b, so we can stay motivated and on track. For these reasons, we need to think about where we are, where we want to go, why we are going and what we need in our rucksack. This means assessing our current strengths and weaknesses as a climber, figuring out the improvements we want to make and what the end point might look like, having good reasons to make the changes and what skills we need to learn along the way.

CHAPTER 1

Psychological skills for climbing

Analysing your strengths and weaknesses

Part and parcel of setting appropriate goals for yourself is having a really clear sense of where your strengths and weaknesses lie as a climber. There are plenty of tools out there which can help you to measure your current technical, tactical and technique skills,[1] but few which outline the main psychological skills needed for climbing. This chapter is all about the key mental skills required for climbing, and how to measure and analyse your starting point and ongoing progress.

WHAT DO WE KNOW ABOUT MENTAL SKILLS FOR CLIMBING?

If you're a climber then you'll know at an instinctive level that what happens in our heads has a large role in predicting the outcomes on the rock. Some research has suggested that psychological skills may have a larger role to play than physiological parameters,[2] but surprisingly there has been very little good-quality research on the psychological or mental skills necessary for climbing. We have anecdotal evidence from elite climbers and coaches, but in terms of good-quality research evidence, this is an area ripe for investigation. We can draw some parallels from other sports such as gymnastics or diving for example, but climbing poses some unique challenges in that it doesn't rely on a routine set of movements, performed in the same sequence over and over again, and indeed any given route may have multiple solutions depending on the style of the climber.

For onsight climbing, the ability to quickly find efficient movement solutions to novel problems is crucial,[3] and we still don't fully understand the range of skills and practices required to develop this ability. It is likely that visual-spatial problem-solving skills are helpful here, but how do we develop them, especially if you are not someone to whom this comes easily? If we are into redpointing, then the ability to memorise a long sequence of complex moves becomes crucial, so what is the best way of developing route memory? These questions have yet to be answered in research terms, though coaches and climbers will have their own favourite ways of teaching this.

There will be many general skills in common with other sports; for example, we know the ability to set good goals is helpful for sport development.[4] We also know from other sports that the ability to manage our emotions is helpful for confidence. However, climbing (and other adventure sports) is classified differently to mainstream sports such as running or other track and field sports due to the perceived risk to the climber. Whilst we may have ropes, gear and belayers to protect us, climbing may often feel like a 'risky' activity, and whilst roped climbing relies upon a solid belay partner, it has a very different feel to team sports with an element of combat in them such as rugby or football for example. So how might the emotional control elements differ for climbers as compared to other sports?

VISUAL INSPECTION SKILLS – ROUTE READING

What do we know so far about the mental skills required for climbing? Elite climbers and coaches agree that what happens even *before* we climb is important for a successful ascent. This includes being able to accurately visually inspect a route and see the potential moves, links and sequences. This skill is likely composed of a series of micro skills – route reading, route memory, rest identification and memory for rests/recovery points, as well as being able to notice and discount irrelevant hold information. In controlled experiments, route previewing has been shown to reduce the number of stops and pauses on a route but not necessarily to directly impact on whether the route was sent or not;[5] this was regardless of the climber's ability level. So there is an argument for practising route previewing regardless of whether you are fairly novice or experienced as a climber, in that you are more likely to select the optimal sequence if you are good at route previewing.[6]

ADAPTABILITY AND CREATIVITY

There is also a vast array of information to be taken into account whilst climbing – variabilities in rock types and holds and therefore movement patterns, environmental changes making conditions different on a frequent basis, and changes in the practice itself – onsight/flash, redpointing, headpointing, seconding, bottom roping, soloing, bouldering and so on. Grading systems provide a very broad-brush categorisation of difficulty, but given the subjectivity involved, they say little about the multitude of variables which will affect you as the climber on that particular route on that particular day. So some ability to perceive all the variables and weigh up their relative impact and how to manage them to their best effect is key.[7] This is both a huge information processing challenge, and requires a commensurate organisation of motor actions in response to the constraints of the route.[8] In simple terms, we could call this the ability to 'break down' a route into all the relevant factors we need to consider, and make sound decisions about how to weigh up and act on all these factors, and adaptability is crucial to this.

FOCUS

Attention and concentration skills have also been shown to be important.[9] Depending on the length of the route, you may need to sustain your focus anywhere from a couple of minutes to 60 minutes for a longish trad pitch, tuning out the potential distractions of other people climbing nearby, changes in weather, wind, caterpillars crawling out of cracks (I remember this being a big issue one year at Tremadog!) and so on! There is also a need to tune into the rock in front of you if you are onsighting or problem-solving on the go, focusing on small affordances/edges that give you opportunities for moves, and the bigger motor control picture of what is happening in your body as you move and how to move and rest for maximum efficiency. It is certainly off putting at that point to have the focus switch to your thoughts or feelings, especially if they are negative or unhelpful.

EXECUTIVE FUNCTIONS

Attention is just one component of what are often termed executive functions. These are higher-level cognitive skills and include attention, ability to switch focus or sustain focus as needed, working memory, self-awareness and self-control, impulse control, problem-solving, planning and strategic decision making. Similar to the conductor of an orchestra, executive functions organise and orchestrate perception, motor responses, behaviour and so on. Executive functions can decline under stressful conditions and impact on effective planning, decision making and complex actions. Not all climbing occurs on a relaxed holiday in sunny Spain; changeable or uncertain conditions such as extreme cold or a sudden thunderstorm, where the stakes are high such as in committing climbs where say you have abseiled in, or perhaps where we feel social pressure or are under par physically, can all impact on the cognitive elements of climbing performance.

It's likely that some climbers have a better underlying ability to deal with the challenges of more extreme environments, but equally practice and training can help with preparation and adaptation. I can clearly remember being a guinea pig for a trainee instructor on one of the wettest Welsh days, trying to climb on the Idwal slabs with water pouring into my sleeve and heading straight to my armpit. Not an enjoyable experience at the time nor one I would have actively chosen, but it did give me a different perspective on what 'good conditions' consisted of, a practice run at problem-solving in a difficult environment, and the knowledge that I could probably still climb during a cloudburst.

PSYCHOMOTOR SPEED AND ACCURACY

You don't need to be a specialist speed climber to find speed useful; some of the finest climbers around at the moment are also the speediest. North Wales–based pro-climber Pete Robins is a blink-and-you'll-miss-it onsight climber, Adam Ondra is well renowned for climbing hard sport routes incredibly quickly and Eric Horst's analysis of Margo Hayes's ascent of *Biographie* (5.15a) showed that she actually spent more time resting than climbing, with the sequences being sent quickly and efficiently. Of course there were some great examples in the 2020 Tokyo Olympics where 'specialist' speed climbers were no slouches in boulder and lead. Being able to perceive the visual information in front of you fast and respond quickly with your body can certainly be a useful cognitive skill for onsight climbers,[10] with a quick reaction time helping to perhaps mitigate for any shortfall in fitness or stamina. Becoming accurate at speed but also being able to vary your pace for optimal effort across the route or problem is beneficial. We know from research that expertise in climbing can be seen via more dynamic movements, shorter climbing times, fewer exploratory moves and quicker decision making.

CONFIDENCE

Self-efficacy,[11] which is having confidence in our ability to climb a particular route or problem, has been shown to be an important psychological 'skill' for climbers,[12] and certainly one which can be cultivated. That inner confidence comes more easily to some people than others; there is a whole chapter later on developing confidence, and it links neatly to having a sense of mastery and improvement, a key motivator for many climbers. Having a strong sense of self-efficacy has been linked to the ability to take apparent risks when climbing, and overcome the inner warning system which usually keeps us out of high-risk situations[13] – that is to say, the higher our sense of inner confidence for completing a route, then we are able to take more risks when climbing. Having the ability to manage our nerves, anxiety or fears when climbing is often the biggest barrier to developing that inner confidence despite maybe many years of climbing experience, and the issue that most of my clients come to me for help with. This is covered later on in this book.

MANAGING YOUR EMOTIONAL RESPONSES

There are other mental skills which I have found to be helpful which haven't yet been researched much in climbing. Here, what we know comes from shared experiences amongst climbers and from other sports. This might include being able to manage your stress levels and get your arousal and activation levels just right for the route in front of you, being able to tolerate frustration and failure, and the ability to learn quickly from 'mistakes' or attempt failures. And of course, crucially the ability to manage feelings of fear around potential falls. It is likely that many of these latter skills contribute to a feeling of self-efficacy, since having a sense of emotional control is a key part of confidence.[14]

Your internal emotional state will also influence your ability to perceive the usability of the holds in front of you. If you've ever been run out on a route, searching desperately for a piece of gear, you'll know that sometimes they only appear when you find a decent hand or foothold, and decent hand or footholds only seem to appear once you have your gear in! Anxiety tends to focus our attention on the present threats to our safety and fix our minds on opportunities for stability, and this means that we may miss holds, moves or gear placements by taking shorter moves and keeping our eye gaze closer into the body.[15] So being able to recognise and dampen down anxiety, as well as taking active steps to mitigate the tunnel vision caused by stress, will have a positive impact on performance.

MOTIVATED FOR IMPROVEMENT

Intuitively we know that being motivated is important for good climbing performance, but it is really motivation for mastery that is a mental skill. It can be hard going, throwing yourself at problems, routes or even moves that you find difficult, and experiencing multiple failures. It can feel bruising to plateau in performance, and it is no wonder that many climbers choose to stick with what they know, repeating routes they can already climb or sticking to what's well within their comfort zone. However, climbers who are motivated for mastery will work on their weaknesses, improve their movement patterns and technique, and seek out experiences that lift their learning. This is both a mindset shift for many climbers and a set of effective behaviours for improvement. We can be super-motivated to climb, but not necessarily motivated to improve, challenge and test ourselves – neither is 'better' than the other, but if you want to be a better climber, then embracing failures as part of the learning experience and seeking out opportunities to 'fail' is key. Aligned with this, we know from general sports research that the ability to set effective goals will aid improvement,[16] and this in turn requires motivation to stick at them. Shifting from an outcome mindset (did I send it or not?) to a mastery mindset (what did I learn? how can I improve?) is an important mental skill for climbing performance improvement.

ASSESSING YOUR CURRENT PSYCHOLOGICAL SKILLS

If you are using this book, there is a good chance you are aware of some of the blocks to your climbing. However, considering the whole range of psychological skills that are helpful for climbing well, getting a sense of where you are now, where your weak spots are, as well as where your strengths might lie, is really important. The tool below provides a quick and easy way to measure where you are now and track progress over any training programme. It has not been validated by research, but will give you a subjective and personal yardstick for your own headgame skills. There may also be some very individual tactics personal to you that you want to add in there. Measuring now, just as you might do with a finger boarding programme, and at regular intervals as you train your brain, will allow you to see the impact of any training you do. It will also allow you to capitalise on the strengths you already have. If you train your weaknesses, and play/climb to your strengths when you want to send, then you are maximising your efforts and inputs.

Climbing psychology skills assessment

Shade in the boxes to give an idea of how you compare yourself now to where you would like to be – the closer to 10, the nearer you are to where you would like to be. It might help to compare yourself to someone at the level you want to be at already.

Area	Specific skill	1	2	3	4	5	6	7	8	9	10
Emotional control	Ability to stay calm under pressure										
	Commitment to making a move (above gear or bolts)										
	Enjoyment										
	Motivation										
	Managing fear and anxiety										
	Confidence										
	Constructive self-talk										
	Willingness to have a go at or above your onsight grade										
	Managing anxiety before a big event (competition, project lead)										
	Self-compassion/ kindness										
Cognitive skills	Ability to focus (concentration)										
	Visualisation and imagery										
	Creating conditions for flow										

Area	Specific skill	1	2	3	4	5	6	7	8	9	10
	Route reading										
	Problem-solving										
	Ability to focus when others are watching (e.g. in competition)										
	Learning from mistakes in a positive way										
	Organisational and decision making skills when climbing										
Psychomotor skills	Body tension control & body awareness										
	Speed										
	Accuracy										
	Adaptability and creativity in movement and problem-solving										
	Spotting affordances – noticing helpful information about holds and how to use them										
Habits and behaviours	Goal setting/planning										
	Ability to take note of your own needs (assertiveness)										
	Ability to recover from mistakes										
	Sticking to a training plan – long-term motivation										
	Being able to adapt your training plans										

Area	Specific skill	1	2	3	4	5	6	7	8	9	10
	Motivated by improvement – mastery mindset										
Tactics	Mental warm-up										
	Planning gear placements										
	Planning rests/rest–effort balance										
	Having a back-up or get-out plan										
Health and climbing for the long term	Health/taking rests										
	Ability to adapt and maintain new habits										
	Diet and positive body image										
Others factors important to you*											

If there are certain mental factors which are important to your performance and they are not listed here, please let us know as you will be helping to add to the body of research on climbers!

It's also important to be aware that how we are feeling currently about climbing and life can colour our self-assessment. For example, if you are feeling downhearted about aspects of your life outside of climbing, it is possible that this might cause you to negatively evaluate your climbing abilities also. For this reason, I would advise you to also ask someone you trust, who you climb with regularly, for feedback on your climbing. You can even ask them to complete the same assessment tool and discuss any discrepancies in the results, and there is a free copy available to download from the Smart Climbing website.[17]

Another tool which is also now readily at our disposal is video – can you get someone to video you climbing a route or problem that is in the style you want to be good at, and then play back and analyse your performance? Look for hesitations, times you looked down perhaps rather than ahead, areas where you felt you were climbing well or poorly, and then try to remember, what was happening in your mind at the time? Our memories are not always accurate! A great example of this is the video of Mina Leslie-Wujastyk climbing Careless Torque; a fantastic high ball, technical boulder problem at Stanage Plantation, which you can find on Vimeo. In the narrative, on the last attempt before she sends, Mina recalls that she thought she had the problem in the bag; however, if you watch the video back, you can see that she hesitates with her right hand and dips her head, just before she falls off. That same hesitation and look down does not happen on the attempt when she sends; so even pro climbers can sometimes struggle to recall their climbing accurately!

Measuring your progress at regular intervals (such as fortnightly or once a month) and comparing will help you to track your progress, and also to see that despite any inevitable ups and downs day to day, overall, you are (hopefully) improving. This is great for motivation and helps to prevent one bad day derailing you. It also allows you to change tack if something is not working. You can also be pragmatic about where to start with mental skills training, and choose a skill which fits best with what you want to climb. Alternatively, choosing the low-hanging fruit – the skill which you think will be easiest for you to learn, or, if you are feeling particularly committed, perhaps start with your weakest mental skill as working on this will bring the maximum gain for your efforts. These principles also apply to physical training, and though not many climbers are systematic about measurement, it can certainly enhance the training process.[18]

In summary, combine as many sources of information as possible to assess yourself on each of the mental skills for climbing, so you can make the assessment as objective as possible. There is also a more specific tool for analysing any anxiety you may have about different climbing situations, in the section about fear of falling. Measure your progress on a regular basis, and try graphing it up to track your development over the longer term.

LINKING YOUR ASSESSMENT TO GOALS

Now that you have a thorough understanding of the mental skills you need to improve your climbing, and a sense of your current skills and abilities, you can make the link to your performance and process goals, and then to action plans. For example, let's say that you want to be good at onsight trad climbing, but you struggle with route reading. This is one of your weakest mental skills and you have scored it as 4/10 on the assessment above.

First, think about what level of route reading ability you think you need for your outcome goal/desired trad route. Can you inspect most of it from the ground, or will you need to think on your feet as you climb because many of the holds are hidden? Is there one crux, or a series of sequences you need to get right? How many moves do you think there are between rests or pauses? This will tell you roughly how many moves you will need to read and recall in any one go. Could having route reading skills at, say, 6/10 be enough, or will you need to be top of your game for this route?

Let's say that 6/10 will suffice for the route you have in mind. Now you need to figure out how to move from 4 to 5 out of 10, and then from 5 to 6 out of 10 for route reading. Do you need to practise the 'reading' element, or the memorising element, or both? This may seem like a deep level of detail, but in my experience, the more closely you can link your skill development actions to your goals, the more likely you are to see the relevance and stick at them. Key questions to ask yourself are, why do I need to improve this skill, what are the components of this skill, and how will I improve each of them. This will allow you to create really specific goals for yourself, and therefore to quickly see some progress.

Climber study: Steve

Steve is happily onsighting around VS, but wants to develop his red pointing skills for an upcoming holiday to Kalymnos, where he has a much harder route in his sights. The line caught his eye a couple of years ago, and its long and sustained, and slightly beyond him grade wise at the moment. Analysing his mental skills, the key problems we discovered were that Steve tended to 'go off the boil' after around 10 metres, losing focus, something which didn't tend to happen in trad as he had opportunities to pause and regroup whilst he placed gear, which naturally broke the routes down into chunks for him. Also, Steve rarely practised refining sequences or memorising long sequences of moves. For both of these skills, Steve scored himself at around 4/10 and figured he needed to move up to around 8/10 for focusing, and around 6/10 for memorising a sequence, since the top part of the route was fairly straightforward to read in that there were few options holds-wise.

Looking at what options were available to him for training, his nearest indoor wall was a bouldering gym and there wasn't a lot of sport climbing nearby. Steve was a bit gutted to figure out he needed to start bouldering – not something he had considered as a trad climber! – to get some experience at working finding efficient movement sequences. I suggested he played the 'add a move' bouldering game with a bunch of friends at the wall to try to make it fun! This also allowed him to build up the length of sequence to memorise gradually. At the beginning he used some videos to help him recall the sequence, as well as trying to tell his partner what he had just done to encode the patterns. He worked at finding three different solutions to each boulder problem (efficiency), and building up from memorising a sequence of five moves to around ten moves over a period of around two months (memory). He also spent time practising his focusing skills when he climbed outdoors, trying to stay in the moment using visual and sound cues for increasing amounts of time rather than going into 'autopilot' mode! We realised through discussion that Steve was probably erring on the side of 'too easy' in his trad climbing which was enabling him to switch off to a degree, and that upping the difficulty by choosing routes which were more challenging to him, or with a crux nearer the top, at the same grade would encourage him to keep his mind on the job for longer.

SUMMARY

We are still learning about the key mental skills required to be a good climber, and it is likely that different skills come into play according to your experience level and personal factors. Having a good understanding of your own mental game strengths and weaknesses will allow you to set really specific and relevant goals, where you can see direct links between your training efforts and the route or project you want to send. This makes progress much quicker and helps to keep motivation higher, as you know that each mental skills training session you complete will move you closer to the end goal you really desire. Measuring and tracking your progress through graphs and tick boxes can help you to see the big picture and not allow the odd down day to knock you off course, but it also lets you quickly see when your training efforts are not working for you and change tack if needs be. Whilst this can feel like a lot of detail and effort, in my experience this is time well spent and pays dividends in motivation and effectiveness.

CHAPTER 2

Dreams, values and goals

Not just goals then?! There are loads of articles out there which tell you how to set a SMART or SMARTER goal,[1] but not all goals are created equal, and if we are an improvement sort of person, we can end up setting goals we think we *should* achieve, rather than goals we actually *want* to achieve. So goal setting needs to be broader than just a specific, measurable, achievable, realistic and time-bound goal. We need process goals and outcome goals (more on this later); we need to ensure our goal will fit with our values and lifestyle, and that it also inspires us. If you are tempted to skip this section thinking, I already know I want to climb E2, then stick around, because that type of goal is a sure-fire way of not climbing E2 and losing a stack load of motivation along the way.

FINDING YOUR 'WHY'

Let's start with some inspiration: when you first started climbing, what was it that you loved about climbing? What got you hooked and coming back for more? I'll bet it wasn't a set grade, rather a question of how hard could you climb if you really tried? Maybe you loved the movement, the improvement, the surroundings, the shared sense of purpose with your climbing partner, or perhaps it was the failures that drew you back every time to see if you could latch that hold next time? I'll wager you approached each climb with a sense of curiosity, perhaps even trepidation 'I wonder if I can do this one?' or 'That looks a bit tough, can I do it?' At the outset, it's unlikely that you thought 'I should be able to climb F6b', at least until you had been climbing a little while and got your head around the grading system.

At some point, nearly all climbers subvert their curiosity and start predicting what grades they can and can't do, and most likely end up on slightly circular training programmes where they simply try to go up a grade or two, but without a really good reason why. They may be motivated to fingerboard for a few weeks, but pretty soon the motivation drops off, they go back to old habits and remain wallowing on a plateau of performance.

I'm not saying that wanting to improve is a bad thing; indeed, mastery is good predictor of intrinsic motivation, one of the more powerful motivators of human behaviour. But grade-/number-based improvement tends to reduce this wonderful and varied sport we love into a kind of tick-box exercise. If we want to keep our motivation high for improvement, then we need to connect with the things we love about the sport. Which routes or problems did you love doing and why? Which were your best days out climbing? What lines have you seen that you really like the look of? What type of climber would you like to be? What style of climbing do you most enjoy? Which routes or problems have grabbed your attention so much that you keep returning to them over and over again, either literally, or in your mind when you are home from the crag? It is always fascinating to me that even climbers who get really scared often keep climbing *despite* high levels of fear and unpleasant experiences – if that's you, what keeps drawing you back to climbing, time after time? Take some time to write down what type of climbing, route, project or problem really inspires you. There are some prompts and ideas below.

Exercise: Finding your 'why'

Take some time to think back to your best day's climbing. Close your eyes and try to remember as much detail as you can about the day. Who was there? What was the weather like? What was the scenery like? What kind of climbing were you doing? When you have a clear picture in your mind, try to feel in your body how you felt that day. What kinds of thoughts and feelings did that day inspire in you? How did you feel during the climbing itself, and afterwards? What made that day so brilliant? Try to go beyond just the idea of sending something, and into what that send gave you, even if you ticked off a long-held dream route or project. What words do that day bring to mind now? Make a note of what climbing 'gives' you.

If you have a clear idea about what climbing means to you, then keeping any changes or training clearly linked and connected to this 'why' will help you to keep going when motivation dips.

VALUES

Next, we need to think about our overall values and lifestyle. How does climbing fit into the rest of your life? You'll already know that if you are working, have a family or caring responsibilities, then time is limited and even if climbing is your passion, it can be hard to fit in more than one or two sessions a week, even aside from the vagaries of the weather! But if push came to shove, which parts of your life come first? The reason for thinking about this is to be realistic about what you can fit in and achieve from your climbing, when and where you have room to manoeuvre, but also, are you content with the life you have? Does it fit with your internal sense of purpose? Or are some of the day-to-day things you do moving you away from what is most important to you? For example, you may be watching trash TV in the evenings because you are too tired for much else, but does this fit with your value of improving your climbing?

Now is the time to get really honest about what is nourishing and nurturing you (which does include rest and recuperation!), and what is just filling time, perhaps because you don't have a clear idea of what it is you really want to do or what is important to you (there is a time audit in chapter 3). Sometimes, we may fill our time with scrolling or surfing because we are avoiding difficult things in our life, which is ok short term, but longer term will be moving you away from what gives your life meaning and purpose. Being clear about your values is your *why*, and research shows that having a strong *why* that is personal to you (not what others think you should do) will help you stay motivated longer term.[2] From a behaviour change perspective, having a strong value base will help you to stick to your plans when the going gets tough[3] and if you need to choose say between trying something tiring, unpleasant or even aversive, and doing what feels familiar and comfortable (like sitting on the couch watching another episode of Friends!).

Values are not to be confused with achievements or activities. Values are qualities, morals, ethics or ideals that you hold dear to you, and we need to think about them in the broad sense of our life, as well as in the more specific sense in relation to climbing. For example, if you value contentment in your life in general, would this value be at odds to having a value of continuous improvement in your climbing? If time with family is your top priority, how will you reconcile this with fitting in enough climbing training time to meet a climbing value of working hard? Mapping out your values in life and climbing will help you identify any possible points of conflict that need resolving, as well as helping you to align your goals with your values, giving them that extra stickability. It is worth taking some time over the exercises below, to really get a deep sense of what is important to you, before embarking on any sort of training programme, so you know it is really worthwhile.

Identifying your values – '80yrs old' exercise[4]

The purpose of this exercise is to try to clarify what is most important to you, what gives your life meaning and purpose, to ensure that any goals you set later on are consistent with those values. Close your eyes and imagine you are 80 years old and looking back at your life. Your friends, family and close colleagues have turned up to your birthday party to celebrate your life. Try to picture who will be there and what memories they are sharing of you as you speak to them all. Perhaps some might give a speech saying what they most admire about you and sharing thoughts about your qualities, and giving anecdotes which illustrate what they best like about your personality. What might you want them to they say? Spend some time really imagining yourself in the future, looking back with friends on your life.

1. *How would you like to be thought of?*
2. *Which qualities in yourself are you most proud of?*
3. *What qualities do you wish you had spent more time developing?*
4. *What has given you satisfaction and contentment?*
5. *Who is a role model to you and what qualities in them do you admire?*
6. *What do you wish you had done more of and why?*
7. *What do you wish you had spent less time worrying about?*
8. *If you had no worries about money, love or recognition, what would give you a sense of purpose in life?*
9. *When do you feel most alive and most 'like you'?*
10. *How would you like to be remembered?*

From the answers above, what common themes do you notice? Can these be condensed into around five to seven core values? For example, if there is a long list of achievement-related goals in there, then that tells you that a sense of achievement is important to you, and why a lack of perceived progression might be demotivating. But it is also important to ask why achievement is so motivating – is it what you learn, or is it the sense of competence? Think of your values as guiding principles for your life – they should give you a framework to help you decide how to spend your time and your priorities when faced with decisions.

There are lots of other exercises to help you think about values. For further reading in this area, check out the book *The Happiness Trap: Stop Struggling, Start Living,*[5] by Russ Harris.

FROM LIFE VALUES TO CLIMBING VALUES

Now let's think about climbing specifically. The exercise earlier in this chapter where you recalled your first experiences of climbing should give you some good clues about what you want your climbing to stand for, what it is all about for you and what qualities would make a great day out climbing. The exercise below invites you to draw out your climbing 'coat of arms' – three to five core elements which make climbing the right sport for you and keeps you coming back to it, time after time.

Exercise: Climbing coat of arms

In the shield below, draw out your top climbing values – what words or pictures really sum up what climbing means to you, and what you want climbing to stand for in your life? This is your climbing coat of arms.

Now you have a sense of your broad values and your climbing-specific values, it is time to look for commonalities, cross over and divergence or conflict. Take a look at the example below, where Tesni has mapped out both sets of values side by side and compared the two:

Example Values Comparison: Tesni

Personal values	Climbing values	Notes
Family closeness	Shared experiences with my partner and friends	Time conflict and lack of baby sitter an issue. Maybe we need to have family crag/exploring days? Mapping out what time I spend with who might highlight whether I'm feeling guilty for no reason?
Education and learning	Improvement and development	These tie in nicely, but I need to understand why I am doing something to make it more interesting
Minimising impact on environment	Being outdoors	No wonder I find climbing gyms de-motivating! Also need to think about how to weave climbing into journeys already taking place as unlikely to drive to venue unless already out in the car
Helping others	Fun and lack of pressure	Need to think about time balance for myself vs. others or possibly I can support my friend to also work on her fear of falling to align with this value?

So for Tesni, her climbing priorities are going to be shared experiences, outdoors where she can gain a sense of improvement without pressure. It is unlikely that she is going to stick to a time-heavy programme which involves lots of gym hours, since this just doesn't align with her values either personally or climbing-wise. You should be starting to get some ideas about what might work for you motivation and training plan-wise, and where you are likely to come unstuck. This section should also give you some ideas towards developing an outcome-based goal – an end point that could be a dream route that will inspire you by stretching your climbing whilst at the same time fulfilling your climbing values. Make some notes as you go along, as you'll be needing them when we put everything together at the end of this chapter.

GOALS AND ACTIONS

Outcome-based goals

Now is the tricky bit where you need to synthesise the skills, time and motivation you have at your disposal, to pick out an outcome goal that is just beyond where you are now. Ideally you should just choose one – it is fine to keep another couple of dream routes on the dream list, but committing to one outcome goal tends to work best.[6] Outcome goals are just that – the outcome or end point you want to achieve. Ideally this will be a route or problem that really inspires you, not a grade-based goal, because you will find it easier to pick out the specific skills you need to develop in order to send your dream route. There is a world of difference between the skills you need for an HVS at The Roaches, versus an HVS on slate, for example, so goals which are solely based on grade can be unhelpful in that they don't help you to operationalise all the skills you will need for a particular route at that grade. Many climbers turn to mental skills training when they want to break through a grade barrier, so here I would suggest you use the analysis from the assessment section to think about what strengths you have in your climbing. You can use these for goal setting, for finding a route which capitalises on your strengths, as well as aligning with your values in terms of having the type of experience you might enjoy or find satisfying.

However, solely setting outcome-based goals is a mistake, since whether you actually send the route is often out of your direct control.

Whilst this might not be apparent for easy routes that you feel are well within your typical climbing ability, think for a moment about all the variables which are outside of your direct control when climbing a route at your limit. Weather, rock quality, gear availability and whether someone else is on the route can all interfere with your ability to complete the route. What is within your control, however, is how you climb it, and the tactics, skills and techniques you will utilise to get the job done. This is where different sub-types of goals – performance goals and process goals – come into the equation.

Exercise: Dream big

Close your eyes for a moment and think about all the crags you have visited, guidebooks and coffee table books you have devoured, videos you have seen and routes you have witnessed other climbers achieve, or routes you have tried but been spat off. Which grabbed your attention and filled you with a sense of excitement? Which did you watch, willing the climber to get to the top? Which routes were just the most beautiful lines, with the kind of moves you loved to make? And which were at around 5 out of 10 on the do-ability scale at the moment? Could one of these routes be your outcome goal?

Performance goals

Your next task is to audit that route or problem. What techniques will you need to use? What tactics and technical skills? What mental preparation strategies will help you? What psychology skills will you need on the route itself? These are your performance goals.

A performance goal is a benchmark skill or marker along the way towards the outcome goal, and it should be directly under your control and concrete enough to measure in some way. An example might be, if your outcome goal is to lead Cenotaph Corner, then one performance goal might be to be able to make 20 consecutive bridging moves. Further performance goals might include: to be able to twist equally to the left and right to grab and place gear whilst bridging; to learn how to have a hands off rest in a corner regardless of how good or poor the footholds are; or to remain calm whilst gazing down between your legs into a 50-metre void.

I often think that setting clear psychological performance goals is trickier than setting physical or technique goals because mental skills are less tangible and therefore less measurable. But one way to do this is to use the subjective measure of a sliding scale of 0–10 and measure yourself against this. In the example above, remaining calm could be translated to 'keeping my anxiety levels at around 4 out of 10' (where 10 is terrified and 0 is asleep); or 'feeling confident at 8 out of 10 whilst looking down 50m into the void'. In some respects, it doesn't matter that this is not an objective measure of your anxiety or calmness, since you are the main judge of whether you have this skill or not, only you know how calm or confident you need to feel to send, and you are only measuring the change in your own skill level.

A really good audit of the physical, technical, tactical and psychological skills you need for the route will help you outline a list of relevant performance goals, and then prioritise the top three to five to hit in training – we'll cover prioritising in more detail in the next chapter, but you can either choose to train your biggest weaknesses relative to the project route (a good long-term approach) and prioritise accordingly, or focus on the three skills you think you will need most on the climb (a good short-term strategy if you have limited time). So with these benchmarks and priorities for training in mind, we then need to turn to *how* to make these goals come to fruition, which is where process goals and actions come in.

Exercise: Setting performance goals

Use the table below to help you to figure out what skills you need to achieve your outcome goal

Outcome goal:	
List three key skills you will need in order to achieve your outcome goal:	1. 2. 3.
What weaknesses do you have which impact your outcome goal?	1. 2. 3.
Current level of skill for techniques needed for outcome goal (0–10):	1. /10 2. /10 3. /10
Three priority performance goals	1. 2. 3.

PROCESS GOALS AND ACTIONS

Process goals outline *how* you will develop the skills outlined in the performance goals section, crucial to this particular project. Each process goal will then need a series of actions in order for you to move from where you are now, to where you want to be. So, in one of the examples above, if the performance goal is to make 20 consecutive bridging moves, and currently we can only make 3 without cramping up, then the process goals outline how we can get from 3 to 20. This might be improving flexibility and the length of time you can maintain a bridged position without getting hip cramp, or it might mean improving leg strength – the process goals and actions will differ accordingly.

A really good process goal will, for say the flexibility skill, specify in SMART format what exercises (specific), for how long and how often (measurable), that are doable (achievable and realistic), and until when (time-bound) you will carry out in order to achieve the flex needed to make those 20 moves possible. For the staying calm performance goal, then the related process goals might include practising looking down between your legs and staying focused on the drop for 5 minutes, twice a week, and gradually increasing the height of the drop you look down over the course of 6 weeks for example. It might also include a process goal of practising breathing exercises for 5 minutes every time you go climbing whilst on the ground for the next 12 weeks, and a further process goal of visualising yourself successfully managing any anxiety on Cenotaph Corner, twice a week at home, for the next 12 weeks. Process goals should be the kind of goals where you can draw yourself a bespoke tick chart (or even a star chart!) and note every time you carry out the action with a tick or star sticker.

You might also need to specify some of the actions you will take to make sure the process goals happen. For example, in order to practise my breathing at the crag, I need to ask my belayer to be quiet for 5 minutes so I can concentrate; I need to make myself a reminder note to put onto my water bottle so I don't forget; and I need to download the breathing exercise instructions onto my phone so I have the prompts I need. Whilst this might sound overly fussy and pedantic, the more time you spend planning what you need to do, then the less likely you are to forget and be derailed by your usual modus operandi. Changing patterns of behaviour and habits is hard work, so to make success as likely as possible, write down your goals and actions, and enlist the support of your climbing buddies. There is more about habit change in chapter 3. Clear process goals and actions lead to a clear training plan, which has a sense of coherence throughout since it is built on a foundation of what is important to you. Motivation to stick to it is therefore intrinsic to the plan.

Exercise: Turning performance goals into process goals/action plans

Once you have your performance goals, key questions to ask are:

What does my performance goal look like in 'real life'/in my behaviours?

How does my performance goal break down into specific skills or actions?

How will I learn the skills I need to reach my performance goal?

Why can't I currently manage my performance goal? What is stopping me?

How do I consolidate my process goals?

What do I need to be able to do consistently in order to reach my performance goal?

KNOWING WHEN TO ALTER YOUR GOALS

As a cautionary word, there are times when too rigid adherence to goals and goal setting can get in the way of performance. Often, it is because the focus is on an outcome goal and there are few clear performance or process goals acting as a foundation for the training plan. Sometimes, it is because life circumstances conspire to make sticking to a training plan too difficult, yet the climber still sticks to the outcome goal and gets frustrated by a lack of progress. The climbers I have worked with have been a determined lot, but often with traits of perfectionism under the surface, they can sometimes flip into obsession. If you find yourself consumed by your goal to the exclusion of other things which you value in your life for long periods of time, then it is probably time to step back for a while, since this is when overtraining, injury or more serious mental health problems can occur.

In non-elite climbers, a healthy level of commitment is characterised by dedication to your training plan, but without feeling distress if you cannot train for some reason, and the ability to enjoy other aspects of your life without feeling resentful that you are not climbing. We all get obsessed by a route or problem from time to time, and find ourselves lying in bed running through the moves, but your commitment to training for climbing should naturally ebb and flow over time, with times given over to training and being goal focused, and times to simply play or even have a break from climbing. Trying to sustain motivation to work on goals for long periods of time is unlikely to work, and it is better to split up your year into sections, with time to train and time to relax. Taking a break at the end of a training cycle is a good idea – you should be itching to get back to climbing, rather than having a sense of forcing it. Two to three months seems to be an optimum time frame to sustain motivation and see the fruits of your labour.

OPEN GOALS

As a final word on goals and goal setting, there are times when SMART goals are not the smartest approach. There is some new and emerging evidence to suggest that, if you are returning to climbing perhaps after injury, a long layoff or even having had a really tough time for a while, then having open goals may be beneficial. Open goals are where you set yourself a challenge to do 'as much as you can' or to see how much you can do and are more exploratory in nature.[7] I have found for climbers where their expectations of themselves are so high that it impacts their performance negatively, then having a more curious and open-minded approach can result in more relaxed climbing and a nice surprise in terms of climbing performance. Hawkins, Crust, Swann and Jackman's (2020) study included a sample of people who were unused to exercise, and they found that for this sample, exercise levels and enjoyment increased with open goals relative to SMART goals; however, this was not true for people who were already active. In my opinion, open goals are often more closely aligned to internal values, and help to move people from outcome-based goals and into process goals, increasing a sense of mastery and hence motivation. The climber study example below touches on these points with a climber where having the right kind of goal was key.

Climber study: Sasha

Sasha had been climbing for around five years and wanted to break the plateau she was currently on at F6b. She was climbing twice a week, but found that every time she tried to lead something at or just beyond her limit, she ended up fluffing moves she knew she could make, and generally powering out through hanging around for too long. She was convinced it was a mental block rather than a physical one and was finding her motivation waning.

During the assessment session, it became clear that having just started a new job, in a new town, she was under a lot of pressure outside of climbing. Her career was really important to her and we figured that most of her mental energies were currently going into this, leaving little left for focusing on climbing. Her climbing values were new experiences, with friends, in beautiful places and she described her best days out as leisurely days at sunny crags, messing about on interesting lines. Although she was really motivated to climb harder to open up new lines for herself, pushing harder at this time wasn't really going to work.

Sasha set an outcome goal of an F6b+ line that had really caught her eye on some nearby limestone. Her analysis of her strengths and weaknesses found that she probably had the moves and stamina to do it, but the pressure she was putting herself under was getting in the way. Her main performance goal was to spend 30 minutes every climbing session messing around on something 'too hard', without any expectation of sending it. Process goals were to find three different ways to climb a section/crux, to step away every time she started to feel determined to send it (since this was the usual cue for pressure), and to have a friendly competition with her buddy to see who could climb sections of the route the fastest. Pretty soon, Sasha was climbing the 'too hard' routes and having more fun in her climbing, and the F6b+ was quickly sent.

TIME FRAMES FOR GOALS

Many physical training guides advocate having seasonal goals, which seems sensible given weather and time dictates across the year. For most climbers, I would advocate having fairly short-term goals, to keep motivation up and to minimise the chance of practice drifting from daily to weekly to, well, not really happening at all. This means the real skill is in breaking down any larger or more long-term goals into smaller goals which can be managed in a realistic and short time frame. Have a good long look at yourself – how long have you managed to stay consistently motivated to train for? You may have a multi-year goal of completing Right Wall for example, but if this is going to take many years progression, unless you are extremely obsessive, it is unlikely that this can be your focus for the next five years when you are currently a severe climber at best. My own opinion would be to think of training or skill focusing cycles in four- to six-week intervals, with a short break in between. So if your goal cannot be completed in that time frame, then you need to break the goal down into smaller chunks. The key point here is to be realistic about your motivation to train or change your habits, the time available to you and what you can realistically expect to change in that time frame.

SUMMARY

Any climbing goals you set for yourself cannot be in isolation from the rest of your life and values if you want to stay committed to them.

Having a good reason why, which is specific and personal to you and aligned with your values is a good basis for goal setting. You can then work on translating your dream route or project, your outcome goal, into performance goals which are under your control and form benchmarks along the way, and process goals, which tell you how you are going to achieve those benchmarks. You may also need to think about actions to take to make sure you can fit these process goals into your life.

Ideally, goal setting is something you do in detail at the start of any training process, but it is also a daily action. Asking, what do I want to achieve today? or what is my focus for this session? is a good way to ensure you get the most out of your efforts. However as the climber study shows, there is a difference between being focused with clear goals, and simply putting yourself under pressure to perform. Having an eye for the performance goals and process goals will help turn pressure into success, and allowing being goal focused to ebb and flow through the year will sustain motivation for the longer term.

CHAPTER 3

Sticking to your mental training plan

Habits and behaviour change

Now comes the hard part! If you want to start a mental training programme, then that will involve changing your current habits and behaviours. Changing behaviour is hard and one of the biggest challenges that psychologists and public health policymakers face. Humans are creatures of habit. If you've ever tried to give up smoking or chocolate for example, or take up a new habit like getting up early to go to the gym perhaps, you can attest to how difficult it is to keep going on willpower alone. There are often additional psychological or biochemical reinforcers for our habits, making them even stickier to change. We tend to forget to take into account that our environment triggers our day-to-day routines, and if we change nothing in our environment then we can quickly forget our intentions and return to our default habits. And that is what often happens – we buy an app, a book or sign up for some coaching, do well at sticking to the new regime during the initial burst of enthusiasm and then, over time, slip back to where we started. Maintaining change is difficult, and I don't want the techniques in this book to be another example of something that was a great idea but ultimately you never stuck to!

There is hope. Humans are capable of making sweeping changes and maintaining them, provided certain conditions are met. In all my years of helping people to make changes, the key is not to overestimate how much willpower you have. Even with a very strong 'why', willpower is a weak and easily expended resource and not to be relied upon! You are going to need as much help as you can get if you want to break out of old patterns of behaviour and into new ones. Think of it in similar terms as using nicotine patches and gum, throwing away all the ashtrays, and avoiding pubs, when you are giving up smoking – that is to say, you are going to need a range of strategies to stick to new and unusual routines. This chapter may feel a bit complicated and very details orientated, but it is important to get into the nitty-gritty of how to develop consistent training habits, if you want your efforts to have a lasting impact.

WHAT DO YOU NEED TO GIVE UP TO FIT IN A MENTAL SKILLS TRAINING PROGRAMME?

The unpleasant truth is that most of us have already oversubscribed our time. The impact of this can often be felt in that uneasy, busy feeling towards the end of the day when we feel we are still 'buzzing' but should be winding down; or in crashing out the minute our head hits the pillow; or in trimming back on our sleep to the bare minimum. Sometimes it manifests as procrastination, because the endless list of things to be done is too hard to prioritise. All this means that if you want to add in a mental skills training programme, you are going to need to take something, or some things, out of your week.

The life values audit you completed in chapter 2 provides a good start-ing point to figure out what is most important to you. Your next step could be to make an audit of a typical week and figure out what you are doing due to necessity (no one else can do this and it must be done), what is aligned with your values and what is simply filling time but adding nothing to your life. There is an easy-to-read primer on finding time for valued activities called *Off the Clock* by Laura Vanderkam,[1] but the main message is simple; it's more effective to cut down on the number of tasks in order to focus on what is important, than simply trying to shoehorn more into the day. This is because it's not just about time, it's also about mental energy required for the tasks and in our increasingly complex world, we spend a lot of our time in mental labour. This cuts down on the amount of mental energy – and willpower – available for mental training.

It's often interesting to compare how we think we spend our time with how we actually spend our time – a quick and dirty way of doing this is to set an alarm for every hour on the hour, and simply record what you were doing at that time as a percentage of the hours in the day. Comparing what you *think* you spend your time doing with what you *actually* spend your time doing can illuminate how much of your time is driven by you and your values, and how much may be reactive or dependent on situational cues (social media and phone use is a good example of this!). You could also think about your ideal week – what would it look like? What are the non-negotiables for your health and wellbeing? What might you want to cut out, things that are not aligned with your values perhaps?

For the purposes of this book, I've assumed that climbing, and improving at climbing, is important to you. It might be that through these analyses you figure out that climbing is not as important to you as some other parts of your life, and that is completely ok; maybe mental training needs to take a back seat for now. Perhaps you realise that there just isn't any extra time available, but you would still like to try to improve, in which case you need to figure out what parts of your current routine – climbing or otherwise – you need to drop in order to fit in some mental training. It's all about making your plans as realistic as possible.

Exercise: Time audit

Have a guess how much time you spend each week (on an average week) doing the following activities. Don't worry too much if it adds up to more than a week's hours at your first guess! Feel free to add your own. Then try to work out exactly how much time you spend doing each one over the course of the next week. Leave the last column for now.

Activity	Time: Guess	Time: Actual	Time: Ideal
Sleeping			
TV/entertainment/computer games			
Social media			
Emails			
Life admin (e.g. bills)			
Shopping			
Housework			
Cooking			
Exercise			
Socialising with friends			
Reading/relaxing			
Work			
Family			
Driving			
Climbing			

If you have a clear sense of your values, try to figure out which activities are in line with your values and which are not. You could try highlighting the ones that are. Then work out

- *Which activities are essential (as in you would get sick or become homeless if you didn't do them!)*
- *Which activities are left?*
- *Are they meeting your needs in some way?*
- *Is this the ideal way to meet those needs?*
- *Do they need to be part of your week at all?*

Now you can begin to figure out what the ideal time to spend on each one is. If you want to make a massive reduction in one area (e.g. social media) be aware that you will need to replace this activity (or habit) with something else that has a similar function for you. Just cutting it out isn't going to cut it!

Now you have completed this exercise, do you have a sense of how much time you can commit to a mental skills training programme? If you have cleared a bit of space and have an idea about what is realistic, next you need to figure out how to keep that space clear for your climbing training (i.e. how to stop old habits creeping back in), and how to create a new habit of regular mental skills training.

HOW TO CREATE A HABIT FOR MENTAL TRAINING

As a general rule of thumb, if we want to change our habits, either giving something up, or instigating something new, we need to think about three components – the cue, reminder or trigger for the habit; the habit itself (our mental skills training programme); and the reinforcer (a type of 'reward') afterwards. If we need to give something up, then we must also replace it with something else with similar cues and rewards – human behaviour does not like a void and it will be harder to resist temptation if you don't have something else in its place.

Some research suggests it takes an *average* of 66 days to change a habit,[2] but there was vast variation within this, with some habits taking a lot longer to embed! In all likelihood it's more likely to be correlated with the number of times you perform the habit, so new actions which happen daily may be easier to embed than less frequent ones. Don't be too ambitious with changes at first; aiming for small, regular and imperfect is better than a great training session which happens once or twice and never again. In the book *Atomic Habits*,[3] there is a neat graph which shows that by improving by just 1% every day for a year it is possible to become 37 times better by the end of the year. Small consistent habits add up, but it's the **consistency** that counts. It can be hard to see the improvements initially when they are so small, until you cross a threshold where suddenly you get that leap in performance. Interviews with great elite athletes time and again highlight that it's the regularity and consistency of their training over years which adds up to what looks like a dramatic breakthrough performance.

MENTAL SKILL TRAINING HABITS – TRIGGERS AND CUES

Starting a new habit is often easier than stopping an ingrained behaviour. Invariably, however, it will mean shifting around what you currently do day to day, or even cutting something out. There are several different approaches to starting a new habit. One entails linking the new training programme to something routine that is already in your day, which gives you your cue or trigger. So, an example would be to do your mental exercises at a specific point in the day, say, after your dinner, and use having your dinner as a cue for triggering the new routine of mental training. You could also try it every time you go climbing for example, starting your mental training before your physical warm-up, when you get to the wall.

The problem with this approach is that it's easy to get derailed. The later in the day you aim to carry out your training programme, the more likely you are to be too tired, and, if you have say a stressful job, your willpower capacity may already be depleted. Think about being at the wall or climbing gym – usually your first 20 minutes or so will be spent saying hi to your friends, getting changed, etc., and if you only have an hour before the wall closes, you are unlikely to use the time left for mental training; instead, you'll just go climbing. So, although in theory this first method sounds like a good idea, it is easy to get derailed and find that four weeks in, you've still only spent 10 minutes practising visualisation despite your best intentions.

A second method might be to try to fit in mental training exercises whenever you can through the day, harnessing small pockets of time whilst you are waiting for the kettle to boil, before a meeting, and so on, based on a thorough assessment of what time you have available in the day. In theory this would likely give you a lot more time periods for your new programme, but the danger here is that without a specific plan, the tendency might be to put it off until later, or to lose track of whether you have done it or not. If you've ever had to take a course of medication involving more than two doses in a day, you'll know it's easy to get confused about whether you have or have not taken that tablet before or after lunch. So although this can certainly work for some people, you do need to be good at seizing the opportunity and well prepared with all your kit for the training easily to hand at all times. Keeping a log of when and if you complete the training programme could be helpful here too so you keep track of whether you have or have not completed your target for the day.

A third method is, if completing some training is important to you, then do it first thing, at the first opportunity during the day. Front-loading your day (or your climbing session) like this with your most important action is probably one of the most effective ways I have found to make sure it happens. This way, you have a specific cue to starting the exercise (getting up, or just after your coffee, or as soon as you arrive at the wall), it's easy to tell whether you have or have not done it, and the day/session has not yet thrown other challenges at you to derail you from your plans. You also get that great feeling of satisfaction, knowing you have ticked off your training before starting your day, which provides a helpful reward or reinforcer. Where many people go wrong is that they try to get up ridiculously earlier than normal and find this is an unsustainable habit. However, changing your morning routine can be a realistic option, if you ease into it gradually – I've had personal success with this, writing this book at the start of the day, five days a week. It was the time I would normally have spent dozing and thinking about getting up, half awake and half asleep, or the time I would have taken over that first cup of coffee, so using it productively felt good and that motivation sustained me through the dark mornings!

Just a note here about remembering to implement your mental training strategies when you are actually climbing for real. Ideally you want to build into your mental skills training programme, cues and triggers that you would associate with climbing or when you need to use this specific skill. For example, if you are practising imagery for a lead climb, then your practice needs to include some triggers that you will have around you when you are actually lead climbing, for example, wearing your harness with your rack on it whilst you practise. This side of cues will be discussed further in the chapters on each specific mental skill, but for now you'll need to bear a few things in mind. This will include equipment (nuts, quickdraws, chalkbags, rope and using these as triggers for certain mental behaviours), internal triggers (for example, a change in your internal state triggers breathing in a particular way), and external perceptual cues (where you want your focus to be when climbing to increase your range of movement possibilities for example). As we go through each mental skill, you'll want to be practising it off the rock, but also to have a keen awareness for what cues and triggers you will need to use this skill on the rock too.

THE HABIT ITSELF – YOUR MENTAL SKILLS TRAINING ROUTINE

Again, it's best to have a specific and time-limited routine in mind, and for this to be realistic. You need to be clear about exactly what it is you are going to do, and to have decided on a focus for the training for this week/month, rather than just thinking, 'I'll do some mental training'. As you embark on your new mental training regime, you might want to dedicate just 5 minutes as a realistic amount of time to fit in your new habit, and do this for a set number of days per week and at a set time of the day. This way, it is easy to know whether you have completed your task, to fit it in, and there will be a defined start and end.

You will want to make it as easy as possible to get started on your task, so that you are not wasting time searching for equipment, instructions or whatever. So, set your intention the night before or before you walk into the wall or climbing gym, decide what you are going to practise, and have everything to hand so you can just get started straightaway. The key here is to simplify things and remove as many barriers to performing your mental training exercise as possible, so everything points you towards it. If you are trying to stop an old habit, then the converse holds true – try to create as much friction as possible so you find it harder to engage in the old habit – for example, if you are trying to cut down on beer and crisp consumption to help your climbing, then putting the crisps on the highest cupboard shelf and not buying any beer for a month is an example of creating friction! Make it easy to do the right thing and hard to do the wrong thing.

This is where your current self should try to remember that your future self will have way less motivation, energy and time available than you think it will! For example, there is never much time in the morning to pack your climbing bag so you can go to the wall straight from work, and you are unlikely to grab a healthy pre-climb snack from the garage because temptation, tiredness and hunger are going to drive you towards the easiest options. So, pack your bag the night before, including your snack, and call your friend to make a firm plan to get to the wall. We consistently overestimate our future willpower, motivation, organisation and time available, so it's not enough to set an intention, we also need to be well prepared in advance. If you can automate any of these actions or use technology to help you (like a text message that recurs 10 minutes after your alarm goes off which reminds you that you want to get up early because you are going to use the time to become a better climber, or using social media blocking apps to help you get to bed on time) then do so. The key message is, take as much effort out of the process as possible.

If you should miss a session, as soon as you remember that you have missed, try to make it up as soon as possible. Avoid thinking catastrophic thoughts such as 'that's it, I've blown it, I may as well quit!' – everyone misses sometimes, the key is to use that feeling of disappointment as a motivator for remembering next time and giving you data to improve your habit triggers. If you can accept that at times you will miss a session, and have a plan for dealing with it so you get straight back onto the programme, then you are less likely to lose heart and quit altogether.

THE REINFORCER OR REWARD

People tend to think of this as some kind of treat they might reward themselves with, at some point in the future ('When I've done a month of creative movement exercises, I'll buy myself that new cam' for example).

There are two problems with this approach; first, that reward is too far off in the future to sustain action today (and also perhaps unsustainable cost-wise!). Second, your future reward is unlikely to be enough of a motivator to do something that feels hard, boring or ego-bruising in the here and now.

If you can make that mental workout pleasurable in some way then do so, but also think about what would give you a sense of satisfaction rather than a pleasurable reward. As mentioned earlier, it could be the satisfaction of knowing that by 8:30am you have already completed your mental training for the day. Or you could take a more visual approach, like a tick on a chart on your fridge door, or filling a jar with a penny every time you complete your new habit (which doubles up as a saving scheme for your cam!). But it can also include taking a moment to savour the benefits of having completed your training – after all, you started this new training habit because you wanted to become a better climber, so take a moment to savour that step on the road to improvement. Any reward needs to be consistent with the overall aim – so rewarding yourself with a lie in at the weekend is probably not ideal if you are trying to set a habit of getting up early.

We know that being intrinsically motivated for a sport keeps us interested for longer[4] – that's when we want to climb just because we love it. But if we become too focused on grades and training for a grade rather than a route or problem as a recreational climber, it can really kill our intrinsic motivation. Intrinsic motivation is thought to derive from a combination of autonomy (choice and control over our actions), competence (mastering a skill, being good at something) and relatedness (social bonding with others). The social element has been found to be a key factor in motivation.[5] This is something that many diet programmes or other behaviour change programmes harness by having group attendance as a cornerstone of the programme, yet climbers can sometimes be a bit secretive about the mental side of climbing. Perhaps there is still some stigma to saying, 'I'm working on my fear of falling'. However, having a partner to train with, to keep you accountable and to give you the odd 'well done' can be incredibly sustaining.

In summary, your reward or reinforcer for your new mental training habit should be both internal – taking a moment to feel satisfied that you have completed the exercise – and external – recording this in some way (a minutes count, a tick in a box or a note on your phone). Adding in the social element by checking in with your climbing partner, doing the exercises together if possible, having a regular slot to ask each other 'how have you done with those exercises this week' can be a big help in cementing the new habit in your mind.

Exercise: Mapping out your new routine

Use the table below to help you identify what you are going to do, when and how long for, noting your cues for action and the reinforcer for your training.

Preparation	Cue	Habit/routine	Reward/reinforcer
What do you need to prepare beforehand? When will you prepare? How will you 'reduce friction' for the training?	What will remind you to start training? When will you do it? How will you know you have done it?	What exactly will you do? How long for? How often? When will you stop? What will you do if you miss a session?	What will you do as soon as you finish? What will you say to yourself? How will you mark/measure completing this session?

PUTTING IT ALL TOGETHER

So, you now know what you need to work on, you have an idea of what is important to you about climbing and your 'why' for committing to a mental skills training programme (or indeed a physical training programme – the principles are the same). You have a sense of the time available to you, and you have distilled an overall dream, into a goal, into some performance and process goals, and then into specific actions that will get you towards that goal. Then, you have identified the best time for you to work on these skills, you know exactly what you are going to work on, and you are clear about the cues and reinforcers for doing so. This might all sound a bit too complicated and involved, but most climbers fail in their mental training not because they don't want to succeed, but because they don't have clear plans, routines and habits – there is simply too much friction to carry out their mental training. Don't be one of those climbers – spend the time needed to become well prepared and embed your cues for training.

The final part of the jigsaw is figuring out *when* you will need to use these new skills, and what cues you will use to remind you to use them! In the heat of the moment, we tend to revert back to earlier patterns of behaviour, and so it's going to be important to practise the *transition* into these new skills, rather than just practising the skills in isolation. For example, if you know you want to work on using visualisation skills just before the crux of a route, then you will need to practise linking them into your climbing. You could therefore practise using the act of placing the last piece of gear before the crux, as a cue to take a moment to visualise the crux. You can even enhance this process further when you are practising visualising the route in your mind at home or at the bottom of the crag, by having your gear on, getting into a position similar to that on the climb, making the action of placing your last piece of gear and then imagining yourself completing the crux.

So, thinking about exactly *when* you will use your new skills, and what will trigger you to use them, and building this into your mental skills practice, will really help you to click into these new behaviours at the right time. There are more ideas in each chapter for the specific mental skill under consideration, but once you have got the skills imprinted off the rock, then you will need to build into your routine cues and reminders for performing the skill on the rock.

Climber Study: Jess

Jess was climbing three times a week during the winter but wanted to add in a mental skills training session. She had a busy and stressful job and found herself zoning out on Netflix once home, desperate to switch her brain off. A time audit showed that she was half-watching Netflix at the same time as scrolling on social media in the evenings. Thinking it through, Jess realised that her evenings were about trying to relax and switch off and wanting to connect with friends but without any energy to do so.

Jess didn't have a whole lot of energy available for a mental skills training programme but she was in desperate need of a way of relaxing that was more effective than Netflix and Instagram for 3 hours! She bought an electrical timer which let her set time limits on Netflix consumption, set some limits on her time on social media using a blocking app and decided to start doing some yoga in the evenings. She put her mat out before she left for work each morning, decided she would do her yoga as soon as she got in after work on the days she didn't climb and set a timer for just 5 minutes initially, after which she was free to Netflix to her heart's content. She was careful to have no expectations of completing a full yoga session, just showing up and doing something on the mat. Soon 5 minutes didn't feel long enough and she graduated to a 10-minute yoga routine. She began to feel less stressed and wondered if she was ready to start a mental skills training programme at the start of each climbing session, again doing it first before starting her climbing. After three months, her chart showed she had completed over 50 yoga sessions and 8 mental skills training sessions. More importantly, she felt less stressed and better able to concentrate both at work and in her climbing. This was motivating in itself.

TAKING A BREAK FROM TRAINING

It is hard work maintaining any kind of training schedule in the long term. Of course, the more embedded habits are, the less resources we need to employ to complete them (think of cleaning your teeth, something that likely happens twice a day, every day, and has done for the last 30 years perhaps). However, with something as costly energy-wise and motivation-wise as a mental skills training programme (or a physical training programme like fingerboarding), you will need to think strategically about when to take a break from it. Sustaining motivation in the long term doesn't mean staying super-psyched all the time, that's just not possible. Instead, your desire to train is bound to fluctuate, and at times we all need a bit of a holiday from structure and routine.

My advice would be to have a planned 'holiday' from the outset. Give yourself long enough to get into the rhythm and routine of training and to start to see a benefit, but not so long as you end up missing sessions and feeling bad about it. For me, 10 weeks feels like a good amount of time to focus on something, and then plan to have a week off with no routines, rules or programmes. Enjoy your break and try not to feel guilty or worry that you have 'broken' your streak. It's less disheartening to have a planned break than find you have missed a bunch of sessions because you *needed* a break, which is guaranteed to make you feel crap about yourself and reinforce any internal narratives about having no willpower!

Restarting your habit can be hard, but take a moment to review your progress, and focus on the benefits of the training you have put into practice already. It's also a good point to review and reflect on your plans – were they realistic, do you need to refine your triggers or rewards and do you want to work on something new or consolidate the skills you have? Remember that you managed to start from scratch before; this time you have more data, skills and you know the knack of getting a good routine going. You can bring all these skills to bear when you restart your next batch of training.

SUMMARY

It's best to be pragmatic and practical if you want your efforts at mental training to be fruitful. Spend some time analysing what time you have available to you and figure out what you need to cut out to find time and energy for working on your headgame. Keep in mind that regular but short amounts of time dedicated to mental training is better than an hour-long session which happens once in a blue moon.

Think about when you are most likely to remember to complete your training and what equipment and reminders you will need; try to make it as easy and natural as brushing your teeth, with a clear cue/reminder for getting on with the training. Remember to enlist some support from your climbing partner or an online group if that's your thing, and be sure to note both internally and externally when you have completed a training session. It can be hard to see progress on mental training, so regularly evaluating where you are up to and ticking off sessions is helpful, and remember to plan for missed sessions and for taking a break, right from the start. Willpower is less reliable than regular routines, plans and consistent triggers.

SECTION 1
Summary

Section 1 has highlighted the mental skills that will help your climbing, given you some ways to assess your current skillset, and to figure out where to put your improvement efforts. For any training, mental or physical, or even if you just want to change something about your climbing, then being clear about what route or problem you are dreaming about (rather than a grade) and the skills you need for that route or problem will give you some focus. Marrying this with a clear 'why' – what you love about climbing (and hopefully your dream route or problem ticks that box) – will help sustain your motivation. This will also lead you to clear performance and process goals, set around the skills you need to achieve your overall goal, and linked to specific actions to take.

If you want your mental skills training programme to succeed, then the most important skill to understand is habit creation and sustaining behaviour changes. Understanding how to create a new habit, how to trigger that new habit and how to really embed your training into your daily routine, and then your new skills into your climbing, means you will be much more likely to have the skills you need at your disposal when you are ready to send. Don't rely on willpower alone – harness environmental cues, routines and support from your climbing buddies to keep you on track.

As with any training programme, measuring your progress at regular intervals will help you see that overall, you are making progress, even if day to day, it doesn't feel like that! Learning and change is not linear, there will be peaks and troughs, so what matters is the overall trend. And if all this seems too fussy or involved for you, remember, mental skills training will only work if you actually do it! Spend time on section 1 as it lays the groundwork for the rest of the book, and the knowledge will also transfer really well to a physical training programme like fingerboarding or stamina training.

Now you are ready to start training those climbing psychology skills, first, by fixing any problems in your climbing headgame, and then by finessing your mental skills.

SECTION 2

Fixing problems in your climbing

Common fears, anxieties and worries

Many climbers have issues with their headgame, the most common of which is a fear of falling. However, 'fear of falling' can be a catch-all term, with many different fears or worries subsumed under it. For some people, it is the fear of falling itself; for others, it is the fear of the fear felt when a fall is imminent; for others, it is a fear of losing control of their emotions in front of others. There can also be worries about trust – in the gear and systems, the belayer and being caught by someone else, or in themselves to not jump off too soon, or to not do something 'silly' like tying their knot incorrectly.

The social side of climbing can also cause problems for some people. Insecurities about climbing in front of other people, of being judged and found wanting, of not fitting into the scene, of not being good enough, can all interfere with climbing performance. Worries about how others perceive you can result in underperforming, but also make experiences like choking under pressure more likely. Choking is where there is a catastrophic failure in your climbing, often just being unable to move fluidly even on easy climbing. Finally, a fear of being judged for failure or making mistakes can also inhibit climbing performance, not only on redpoints or long-term projects as they near completion, but also as a more insipid, background worry, which means climbers may play safe for much of their climbing career.

This section will cover some of the theory behind why these problems occur, how they show up for climbers and practical strategies to manage these worries. The model of anxiety development and maintenance is fairly universal regardless of how the anxiety manifests, and so the solutions will have some commonalities, but there are also some specific strategies for each difficulty.

CHAPTER 4

Introduction to fear, anxiety and worries in climbing

In the cold light of day as we sit around talking about cragging, it can be hard to figure out what is so scary about climbing in the modern era. After all, we have a huge selection of protection available; dynamic ropes, a range of belay devices, thick bouldering pads and well-bolted sport routes, and the figures about accidents suggest that injuries from falling whilst climbing are less common than other causes (e.g. errors during descent). But things change once we get on the rock, despite the best intentions of our rational mind. Heart pounding, sweating and sliding fingertips, disco/Elvis leg, feeling sick, frozen to the spot, swearing, crying – most climbers have experienced fear, nerves or anxiety at some point when they are climbing. There may be different underlying triggers and causes, or the fear may kick in at a different point, but it's rare to find a climber who hasn't been scared out of their wits at least once during their climbing career. The obvious culprit is a fear of falling; however, in my experience, this is not the only worry, anxiety or fear that climbers face.

WHAT ARE WE REALLY SCARED OF?

Fear of falling is the most often talked about and tackled worry for climbers. It's almost as if we forget about the rope, belayer, gear or bolts, or big padded mat below us, and simply imagine ourselves falling into the abyss, with the sensation of falling being the most scary part. However, we may also be scared of landing badly and injuring ourselves. Or it could be that the sensation of being out of control – either through falling, or through losing control of our emotions – is the predominant one. Fear of fear itself is a common theme, when we start to unpick what really scares us. And when we unpick that fear of fear, it could be due to the unpleasant nature of fear, or it could be worrying about the reaction of others to our loss of emotional control. Social anxieties can be a large part of climbers' worries too – worries about being judged and found wanting, of making mistakes and looking foolish, or of failing to reach a predetermined level or bar. Climbers may have a pyramid of worries, underneath what appears to be a simple case of a fear of falling. This is important, since the oft-used falling practice solution will work only for some of these underlying fears.

One way of understanding why we have so many different worries is to think about our emotional systems or drives. We tend to be motivated to move away from threats, towards resources (including prestige) and to avoid anything that will have us cast out from the social group. Climbing may activate all of these drives – climbing well brings us prestige and acceptance from a desired group; conversely climbing badly or doing something 'embarrassing' risks that social acceptance from our tribe. And of course, being up high, making tenuous moves and physically exposed is a somewhat threatening environment to be in, giving rise to the psychological threat of fear. Threats therefore are physical, psychological and social, and all of these may be activated when climbing.[1]

WHAT'S THE DIFFERENCE BETWEEN FEAR, ANXIETY AND WORRY?

There is a lot of variation in the terms used (*rational/irrational fear, anxiety, psyched out, terrified, panic, scared, baulking, choking,* etc.) and which applies when, but to me, it doesn't matter what words you use, what is important is that you think about how it manifests itself for you. I recall abseiling into Castell Helen at Gogarth and passing a climber leading Rap who was hunched over, leaning into the rock, quietly sobbing and unable to move. I asked if they were ok and did they need a rope from above, but they didn't really hear me as they were stuck in their own private hell. Their partner cheerful shouted up, 'don't worry, she'll be fine in a minute!' – they most certainly did not look fine and remained there for quite some time, before eventually completing the route, looking extremely shaky. I can also recall working with a climber who, on entering the climbing wall and seeing it was busy, would clam up, go pale and only attempt boulder problems way below their limit, climbing in a very conservative way when others were around. We are all different, and whilst the physiological mechanisms which underpin fear, anxiety and worry may be the same, they are expressed very differently from person to person and sometimes from situation to situation. This chapter uses an example which is primarily about a fear of falling, but you can use this chapter to think about any situation that has made you anxious, and there are some prompts to help you figure out how fear, anxiety or worry affects you when climbing.

Likewise, I don't believe you need to know which part of your brain is being activated when you get scared on a climb; after all, we cannot tell a particular part of our brain to switch off – if only we had that much control over our brains! However, you do need to know what your body and mind are doing and why, in order to learn how to manage them, so you can safely make a decision about whether to try hard, top out, lower off or bring your belayer up to you. At the extreme end, being in the grip of a panic attack when lead climbing can be extremely dangerous, leading to poor decision making, rushing and regression of climbing ability, which, if coupled with poor gear placement, rope management and a ledgy route, can end in an injury. And injuries aside, it's an extremely unpleasant and aversive experience, which stays with climbers for a very long time, colouring their next climbs and for some, putting them off altogether.

I had my own panic attack when climbing in Pembrokeshire, a route called Inner Space, which starts in a cave on lovely big holds and then makes a traverse in the upper seam of the cave, above a gaping void below. I opted to second this route because I really wasn't too keen on climbing inside a greasy cave (give me salty sea air exposed climbs any time, dark spaces give me the heebies) which was a mistake, because my climbing partner, who was tall and lanky, skipped up the route and back and footed across the upper seam with ease, but put all the gear in at what looked like a comfortable reach for them. As I got into the upper seam, I found that I was too short to back and foot across the void and there were very few options for footholds and none for handholds. It was greasy and I ended up making a precarious starfish shape, straddling across the seam making snail-like progress, and becoming progressively more tense by straining all my muscles to keep me on the wall. When it came to getting the gear out, I simply could not reach and it felt as though any minute, my feet were going to shoot out from under me, spitting me out like a bar of soap and plummeting downwards to be left hanging in the void forever! When I eventually arrived at the belay, I was hyperventilating, shaking and making some strange involuntary noise not dissimilar to the cows who were in the field above. I simply could not do anything other than lean over on the ledge, and it took my partner saying very sharply to me 'come on, tie yourself on quick' to kind of come round. I believe the rest of the route was lovely, but I have no memory of it whatsoever – but the memory of that experience in the cave is burned deep into my mind forever! So, what went wrong and how did I end up having such a negative experience?

The first mistake I made was not really listening to my gut instinct, which told me well in advance this wasn't going to be my favourite climb, and I needed to get on top of the anxiety management from the get-go, which I did not do. Many climbers, when they feel the first tingling of butterflies, simply ignore them or try to suppress them, rather than actively noticing them and using them as a cue to get started on managing their nerves in an active way. As I was belaying, I have no doubt that my breathing pattern began to alter, my muscles began to tense up and I certainly had a lot of negative thoughts echoing around my head. By the time it was my turn to climb, I was already in a state of heightened anxiety, and in some respects it was inevitable that the climb would take a turn for the worst! Whilst a panic attack is at the extreme end of things, the way our bodies and minds respond when anxious, scared or panicking is due to the strong body–mind connection, and understanding this vicious cycle is important for any type of climbing-related anxiety management.

THE ANXIETY CYCLE

We can think of anxiety as a cycle (see below), with a number of interlinked parts – thoughts, feelings, body sensations/physiological reactions, and changes in behaviour. They are often described as part of the fight–flight reaction, but can also include a freeze response. These responses have an evolutionary purpose, to keep us safe from predators by fighting them off (fight), running away (flight) or staying still and hiding (freeze), and so they are pretty hardwired into our system.

I've used my example on Inner Space to illustrate the anxiety cycle. At the end of this chapter, there is a blank anxiety cycle for you to fill out for yourself. As we go through each of the elements of the anxiety cycle, you'll find some prompts to help you fill in your own anxiety cycle. For now, take a moment to jot down the last time you felt nervous or scared when climbing.

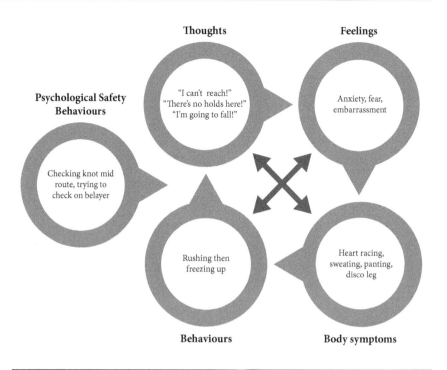

Exercise: Last scary experience

My last scary experience was…

When?

Where?

Who was there?

What were the conditions like?

What happened?

PHYSIOLOGY

Adrenalin and cortisol are the main chemicals released during this cycle, and have the benefit of sending blood to our large muscle groups (like the legs) but temporarily starving non-essential functions such as digestion. An adrenalin burst can last quite a long time though not forever even if it feels that way, but cortisol tends to persist and is associated with longer-term chronic stress. The physical effects of stress hormones include increased heart rate and breathing, dilation of the pupils, muscle tension, a rush of blood and glucose to the large muscles to the detriment of smaller muscles, hypervigilance (tunnel vision or rapid scanning of the environment) and increased focus on threats, all designed to get us ready to fight off a predator, run away or even hide. This is the classic fight, fight or freeze response, hardwired into us to keep us safe.

A climber might feel effects such as getting rapidly pumped in the arms, disco leg, feeling sick, breath holding or panting, and jerky movements. Holds seem to disappear and all we can focus on is how little gear we have or how far we might fall. What worked for caveman therefore is not so helpful for finishing that route!

The physical responses we have are a key part of the anxiety cycle, but given that the mind and body are intimately connected in multiple and bidirectional ways, we can continue to feed the stress with our thoughts and behaviours. The good news is that if anxiety responses are a cycle, then we can implement changes in multiple ways. The main physical changes we experience can be countered with simple physical techniques, allowing us to 'dampen down' the nervous system responses. Exercises like diaphragmatic breathing (breathing from the belly), having a longer, slower out breath, and breathing through pursed lips can all be helpful,[2] and the increased muscle tension can be dissipated with a muscle tense and release exercise. These are discussed in the next chapters. Spend a moment thinking about how your anxiety showed up in your body, last time you felt anxious when climbing.

Exercise: Body symptoms

From your last scary experience when climbing, what sensations did you have in your body?

What happened to your heart rate?

What happened to your breathing?

How did your muscles feel?

What happened to your movement skills?

THOUGHTS

When I first had those butterflies, my thoughts were along the lines of 'it looks really dark up there and I bet it will be hard to see the holds'; 'you know you hate caves, why are you doing this?' and 'how the hell am I going to climb that?!' which I did not voice to my climbing partner and quickly tried to push away with some positive comments. So right from the off, I got into a kind of mental argument with myself, countering radio doom and gloom with things like 'how bad can it be, it's only a VS?!' and 'c'mon, stop being such a wuss!'

Even though I'm a psychologist and know that this is probably the least helpful way of tackling such thoughts, the sight of a dark, looming cave was enough to set off my evolutionary survival instincts (dark cave, greasy, bats, giant scolopendras, getting stuck, etc.), and I quickly spiralled into the anxiety cycle. It's really natural to try to counter the thoughts with logic (after all, we love climbing right?!), but once we tip into the anxiety cycle, we are in the grip of an instinctive, survival process which is designed to bypass the logical centres of our brain, and make action instinctive.

So even though, in the cold light of day or in the pub afterwards, you *know* (with your cortex – your rational thinking mind) that there are no giant scolopendras in the UK anyway and VS is well within your capabilities, at that moment in time as you gaze up at your climb, your logical rational mind is not even in the frame. Instead, you are working with an automatic system honed over hundreds of thousands of years to get you out of trouble, and it isn't going to listen to some new-fangled bit of your brain telling it otherwise. Steve Peters,[3] in his book *The Chimp Paradox*, refers to the cortex as the computer, but the age-old safety system he calls the Chimp, and that's who's in charge right now.

For that reason, rationalising thoughts is not so effective whilst actually climbing. Rationalising exercises (which derive from cognitive behavioural therapy techniques) are best done off the crag or wall. Keeping a thought record (see chapter 9) and identifying common themes of your negative thoughts is useful and once back home, you can use techniques to challenge some of the negative thoughts that occur when climbing. However, when you are actually climbing, time spent in a mental argument is wasted time, sapping energy and shifting your focus off the moves and sequences you need to complete the climb. At this stage, different techniques which help you unhook from the thoughts will be much more effective in helping you to refocus on your body and the rock in front of you.

Another problematic way we tend to deal with negative or anxious thoughts is to try not to think about them, much as I did before starting Inner Space. A simple experiment should show you how futile it is to try not to think a particular thought. Close your eyes now, and try really hard not to think about pink elephants. Keep trying! No, no pink elephants please … do not think about pink elephants. Did you manage it? Even if you did manage not to think about pink elephants for a moment, the chances are that the image or thought will pop into your mind later on. Actively trying to stop or suppress our thoughts may be very difficult to do when we are scared, but also even if effective in the short term, they tend to rebound with renewed ferocity later. This is a kind of mental avoidance, which gives maybe short-term relief from anxious thoughts, but is hard to maintain and ultimately strengthens, rather than weakens, anxiety.[4]

Techniques where we allow thoughts to come and go, without getting attached or hooked by them, might seem harder to get your head around initially or even harder to do, but the research is clear – thought stopping or thought suppression is likely to make things worse and not better with respect to negative thoughts. Try to recall how you dealt with your negative or anxious thoughts last time you climbed and make some notes below.

Exercise: What did you do with your thoughts?

How did you try to manage your thoughts when you last got scared?

How effective was this?

One of the key techniques to use on the rock is to recognise that thoughts are just that; words and pictures in our minds, which may or may not correspond to reality. Unhooking from these thoughts (and feelings, which are just sensations in our body even though they can feel extremely powerful) and focusing on what matters right now will get the route climbed much more efficiently than debating with yourself about how everyone is waiting for you and why are you taking so long dammit! You are aiming to cultivate the observer position,[5] where you are able to observe your thoughts but not get tangled up in them. Exercises to help you develop the observer position are discussed in later chapters.

Exercise: Thoughts when scared

What thoughts did you have when you last felt scared climbing?

What pictures or images did you have in your mind?

What was the worst thing about the situation?

Were there any common themes or thoughts you had over and over?

LOSS OF FOCUS

When we are scared, our ability to focus on the right things (how to climb) decreases and we tend to get sucked into looking at and focusing on the threats (the big drop below me in my case). Our ability to effectively scan for useful holds tends to decrease and we can get either fixated on a hold or a sequence and think that's the only way to move, or find ourselves completely unable to locate a useful hold. Have you ever had the experience of being desperate to get a piece of gear in and finding only terrible holds to use whilst you place it or clip your bolt? And then as soon as you have clipped your rope, you see a huge hand or foothold, or a better way to stand that uses a fraction of the energy you had to use before you clipped! This is an example of the impact of anxiety on our attentional focus, narrowing our field of vision and reducing our ability to problem solve in the moment. For me on Inner Space, had I gone a bit higher up into the crack, it would have been narrow enough to back and foot for a shorty, but in that moment, I could not see that solution. I was fixated on the problems and threats, and not on the potential solutions. Have a think about your focus the last time you felt anxious, and make some notes below.

Exercise: Where was your focus?

What were your eyes drawn to when you got scared?

What was your mind drawn to when you were scared?

Did you get stuck on any particular holds?

Did you miss any holds?

Developing a routine to make sure you focus on the right things when climbing is a helpful way to counter the tunnel vision we experience when scared, and this is discussed later on in this book.

FEELINGS

Our feelings are extremely powerful and designed to motivate us strongly to move away or towards things – away from things that are scary, unsafe or potentially harmful, and towards resources, relationships and status for example. They are hard to ignore, and feel very 'real' to us at the time. But what are feelings really? If you've ever watched a horror film, you'll recall that even though you know you are safe, you can also at the same time be experiencing strong feelings of (hopefully enjoyable!) fear. So there is a physical component to our feelings, and also an interpretative component. Many sport psychology books tell you to simply reinterpret any fear you feel whilst climbing as excitement, and indeed there is a close correlation between the physical component of both feelings, but it is hard to do this when you are 10 ft above your last runner and facing a fall over a couple of ledges. What works in a relatively safe sports context (e.g. track running) may not be so effective when you are in a challenging physical environment. Situational cues play a role, and I believe that being up high or facing exposure adds a hardwired 'unsafe' context to our climbing, meaning that it's easy to tip into fear and anxiety, much harder therefore to reframe it as excitement.

Many people try to cope with powerful feelings by pushing them away or ignoring them. Russ Harris describes this as being like trying to push a beach ball under water – it just bounces back up again, and so it is with our feelings. Much like my experience on Inner Space, where I tried to ignore my initial feelings of trepidation, pretending your feelings aren't there is a sure-fire way of having them bite you on the bum further up the climb. However, it's not about trying to change our feelings either – again this wastes valuable energy and takes focus away from the climbing. Instead we need to acknowledge and accept our feelings, and again cultivate the observer position, and allow our feelings to naturally rise and fall, without getting hooked by them.

Acknowledging and accepting our feelings can be the hardest part, since often climbers have feelings of embarrassment or shame attached to feeling nervous or scared, causing them to try to suppress these feelings. There is a great little video on YouTube of the 'Struggle Switch',[6] which shows how we often layer up our feelings, adding anxiety about our anxieties, and embarrassment about our anxiety, on top of the original emotion. In my case on Inner Space, not accepting my initial feelings meant I did not do what I needed to do to manage my anxiety. Noticing your feelings and taking steps to manage their impact – for example by breathing from the belly, or using a grounding technique to help focus – can happen only if we acknowledge they are there in the first place.

MANAGING FEAR BEHAVIOURS

When we are worried, nervous or scared, our behaviour changes – that's the power of feelings and just what they are designed to do. We are highly motivated to get out of the situation, and to avoid similar situations so we don't have the same experience in the future. Typical fear behaviours include rushing, becoming combative, running away, escaping as quickly as possible, freezing up and avoiding anything vaguely similar in the future. However, avoidance is our main enemy when it comes to overcoming anxiety.

Avoidance is the key maintaining factor in the anxiety cycle; we get short-term relief from the nasty feelings, thoughts or situation, but in leaving and avoiding, we never get to learn to manage our feelings or the situation, and find out that it's actually ok and we can cope. Climbers may tend to stay away from a certain style of route, rock type or hold because they feel nervous, thinking they can work around this without it negatively impacting on their climbing. However, far from not impacting on the rest of their climbing, their comfort zone begins to shrink over time as more and more types of holds or rock or moves get added to the no-list. **Ultimately, we are not avoiding a certain rock type, hold or move, we are avoiding facing up to our fears and weaknesses, and that is what shrinks our comfort zone over time.** What we will need to learn to do is to gradually face our fears by undoing avoidance, in a manageable way over time.

Exercise: Fear behaviours

What did you do when you got scared?

Did you rush, get shouty/sweary or freeze up?

What was the result of your fear behaviours?

SAFETY-SEEKING BEHAVIOURS

Avoidance also gets played out in much smaller ways, which are often not apparent to many climbers or even observers (this is particularly relevant if you are a coach). For example, the most common avoidance I see when coaching climbers is they avoid weighting the rope at the top of the climb until their belayer has pulled the rope in tight and they feel a pull on their harness. Whilst this sounds sensible in practice – wait until the belayer really has you before lowering off – in reality, your belayer should be able to catch you at any point in time on the climb and you should not need to wait for the pull on the harness to drop onto the rope. Here we are avoiding trusting the belayer, and we are also setting up a psychological safety–seeking behaviour, that of only feeling safe when we feel the pull of the rope through our harness. Psychological safety–seeking behaviours are intended to prevent harm or cancel out risk,[7] and therefore give us a psychological sense of safety. However, they serve no real-world purpose and actually mean we can avoid confronting our worries, thereby maintaining our anxiety. For example, if we only feel truly safe when we have the cue of the pull on the harness from the rope, then lead climbing is going to be a difficult task, and we are avoiding trusting the belaying process.

Similarly, many people avoid trying to the point of failure, even when they know they are safe on a top or bottom rope. They may try a move to the point of failure with a tight rope, but feel unable to do so when there is some slight amount of slack in the rope. Another safety behaviour is to kid yourself that you are trying to the point of failure by making a half-hearted attempt at a move, or by saying 'take' rather than trying the move and slipping off. If you never really try to the point of failure, then you are predicting what moves you can and can't do, and playing safe by not trying anything in the uncertain grey area in between.

Other psychological safety–seeking behaviours I have observed include checking the knot multiple times during the climb (the only check you should need is your buddy check at the bottom; could you really re-tie your knot half way up?), looking down to check what the belayer is doing (if you don't trust them to concentrate then you need to have a word or find a new belayer!) and chalking up multiple times when there is already plenty of chalk on hands. These behaviours may not sound much, but they distract from the climbing itself and shift our focus to threats. They tend to reinforce the anxiety because instead of acknowledging the fear, they are attempts to neutralise it and avoid a feared scenario. In time, the goal should be to remove these psychological safety–seeking behaviours in order to face up to some of the uncertainty we try to keep at bay.

We can also have internal avoidance processes – where we try not to think about feared consequences such as falling or things going wrong. These are difficult to observe and can become so automatic that we barely realise we are doing it. It might not seem important and indeed many people use this as a way of coping with worries and difficult feelings, but the problem is that if we can't even think about falling, how can we get comfortable with falling? How are we going to be able to try hard enough to the point of possible failure when the outcome is uncertain if we can't do this first in our imagination? Understanding the multiple ways we try to avoid fear, anxiety or falling and failing is really important if we want to get to grips with the factors that maintain climbing anxiety.

Exercise: Psychological safety–seeking behaviours and other avoidance behaviours

Safety-seeking and avoidance behaviours – tick which apply to you	Yes or no?
Checking the knot whilst climbing (after leaving the floor)	
Chalking up more than necessary	
Checking the belayer is watching whilst climbing	
Additional checks before a difficult move	
Waiting for the rope to be pulled tight before lowering onto it at the top of a route	
Seating and reseating anchors over and over	
Pulling on gear/rope in a quick draw repeatedly to check it's properly seated	

Avoiding hanging on your belay on a multipitch	
Saying 'take' rather than try a move	
Saying 'watch me' before trying a difficult move	
Half-hearted tries on a difficult move	
Readjusting on hand or foot holds when you are already in a stable position ('double tapping')	
Avoiding climbs using holds or rock types you dislike/find difficult	
Avoiding climbing when it's busy	
Avoiding thinking about things going wrong (e.g. falls)	

UNDERLYING BELIEFS

This is where it gets really interesting. Our underlying beliefs tend to give rise to some of the negative thought patterns we experience, and can be detrimental to our climbing. Sometimes, it can be believing it's important to stay in control of our emotions. It may be believing that being scared is being weak, or that it's embarrassing to lose control in front of others. It could be something like you must be good at everything you try, or at an even more basic level, that you don't trust your belayer or the gear for example. Common narratives in the climbing community include things like the harder climber chooses/leads/goes first, or that a certain grade is required in order to be a 'proper climber'. The root beliefs we hold may be broad generalisations, very all or nothing in nature, catastrophic, or based on long-held ideas we developed when part of our family of origin or from within our cultural worlds.

It can be hard to get to the bottom of your core beliefs, but there are techniques to help. These are discussed further in later chapters, but for now, think about what your negative thoughts might be telling you. What is the worst thing about each thought coming true? What ideas and beliefs about fear, anxiety and competence were important in your family and culture when you were growing up; can these give you a clue as how your negative thoughts have developed?

Exercise: Discovering your core beliefs

Think about the common negative thoughts that pop into your mind when you are climbing. What is the underlying worry? What would be the worst thing about that if it came true? Why does that matter? Look for words such as 'must', 'should' 'always' and 'never' – these may give clues to some underlying beliefs.

Do your underlying beliefs make sense to you? Are they true and realistic? Are they still valid and 'in date'? Are they useful to you and your climbing? Having a brief audit of your underlying beliefs is helpful in identifying any which might be working against you, perhaps those assumptions that you have adopted uncritically that are no longer serving you well. This can help you to start to undermine some of the negative thought patterns which recur under pressure.

PUTTING IT ALL TOGETHER

Now you have worked through all the different elements of what happens when you get stressed about your climbing, can you put them together and see how they link together in your own anxiety cycle?

Exercise: Drawing out your own anxiety cycle

Think about the last time you felt scared when you were climbing and your answers to the prompts throughout this chapter. Can you map out your own body symptoms, thoughts, feelings and behaviour changes using the anxiety cycle below

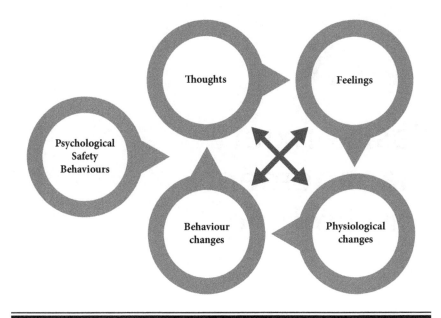

SUMMARY

Accepting that fear and anxiety are a normal part of most climbers' experience is vital in committing the time to learn how to manage that anxiety, to have a better climbing experience. We don't want to get rid of anxiety completely; after all, its purpose is to keep us safe. We just don't want it to be too overwhelming and lead to poor performance. Use your most recent experiences of nerves or fears when climbing to give you some data on what might be going on for you. If you can start to develop your own unique anxiety cycle diagram, it will help you to use the most appropriate anxiety management techniques to suit your situation. If you can begin to see any fearful experience as helpful data to build up a clear picture of how fear and worry affect you, then this can help you begin to turn the tide on anxiety when climbing.

CHAPTER 5

Basic anxiety management for climbing

Now you have a sense of how anxiety affects you when you climb, you can begin to work on making it more manageable and bearable. It's not realistic to expect it to disappear entirely – if we had no fear response, then we would likely take some pretty extreme risks. The challenge, though, is to be able to maintain an accurate appraisal of risk, at the same time as finding the optimum level of physiological and nervous system arousal, so that we can climb to the best of our ability.

HOW REACTIVE TO STRESS ARE YOU?

Everyone is different in terms of their reactivity to stress and anxiety-provoking situations, and indeed, everyone is different on different days. Our underlying reactivity or arousal levels are likely dependent on a combination of genetic factors, early learning and our current stressors. We know that some babies appear laid-back, and some appear much more sensitive, long before they have been exposed to socialising influences, pointing to a genetic component to underlying temperament.[1] So, for example, if you have anxious parents, it's possible that you have inherited a genetic predisposition to being more reactive to stressors. However, it's also possible that you learnt to be more risk-sensitive or risk-averse by watching your family's reactions as you grew older. In all likelihood, being reactive has been a helpful evolutionary strategy – after all, our ancestors who spotted danger quickly would have been the ones to survive, and their offspring would have copied them and benefitted from being threat-aware. However, that previously helpful tendency is often less than helpful in a modern context. Have a think for a moment – do you react quickly to stress or perceived threats, or are you a fairly laid-back sort of person? How did your family react to worries, stress or risk?

Our current life situation will also have a bearing on our underlying arousal level for climbing. If you are in a high-stress job for example, then it's possible that you have high levels of stress hormones circulating, and that can increase your general arousal levels. The saying 'the straw that broke the camel's back' gives an indication that if you have a lot going on, then it doesn't take much to tip you over into too much stress, anxiety or panic. Having an awareness for how we are feeling and our current load or demands is important for balancing the degree of challenge, according to our level of internal arousal. Having an understanding of your general day-to-day reactivity also adds important data to the picture.

WHAT'S THE RIGHT AMOUNT OF AROUSAL FOR CLIMBING?

You may have heard it said that some stress is good for you and necessary for optimum performance. This is a bit of misunderstanding, in that it is actually the right amount of nervous system *arousal or activation* that is good for performance; stress is rarely good for performance, since stress, by definition, is unhelpful levels of arousal or activation. Having a good understanding of your baseline level of arousal is helpful in order to find your sweet spot for performance, remembering to factor in day-to-day variations due to conditions, tiredness, situation or external stressors.

For many sports, athletes will talk about getting pumped up to get into the zone for optimal performance, and sometimes climbers think this is what they need to do as well. For relatively simple tasks with repetitive components like say endurance running, then getting psyched up is helpful to hit the right level of physiological activation. However, for complex tasks like climbing with lots of variables affecting risk and complex and non-routine movement patterns, we typically need less physiological arousal to hit the performance zone. We often talk about getting psyched up for a route, but in my experience, many climbers need to learn how to 'psyche down', dampening down their nervous system responses and their internal arousal levels, to perform at their best (see Figure 5.1[2]). The techniques in this chapter are designed to tackle all aspects of the anxiety cycle to help hit that performance sweet spot.

It's important to bear in mind all the things that might contribute to your underlying arousal levels on any one day, in order to take them into account. A relaxed day, a trusted partner and great conditions at a roadside crag will feel very different to squeezing in a route after work in fading light

FIGURE 5.1 *Yerkes-Dodson Curve, Adapted from Slavin (2018)*

and windy conditions, at an exposed crag with someone you just met off a social media forum, for example! The more stressors you have going on, the more time you may need to take to dampen down the physiological arousal before getting on that route, and you may need to adjust your plans altogether if you find that you are someone who tips into high anxiety very easily. But the first step of anxiety management is weighing all the factors that might affect your anxiety on a particular day and trying to mitigate them. For the long term, it's better to be slightly under your sweet spot rather than becoming too activated/stressed and descending into a big performance decline – to build confidence we need repeated positive experiences.

Exercise 1: Factors affecting your own arousal/anxiety levels

Think through all the following headings – which of these tend to bother you and increase your stress levels?

Internal (e.g. stress, tiredness, hunger, heat, cold, time of day)	*External (e.g. weather, exposure)*
Social (e.g. partner, people watching)	*Route and rock characteristics*

Bearing these factors in mind will help you to pick a challenge that is appropriate given your arousal levels on that particular day. For higher-stress days, opt for something easier rather than 'forcing' yourself to carry on regardless. This need not be forever; as you learn how to manage your anxiety, you can start to work with slightly higher levels of arousal, activation and variability in the factors above. But for now, try not to fight a fire on all fronts – if you have high levels of stress in all the areas above, then dial down the difficulty of the climb, and/or devote more time to dampening down your nervous system activation. I like to imagine an old-fashioned hi-fi system, with dials that let you adjust the treble, bass and balance – it's a good analogy for adjusting the levels of challenge in each of the areas above, so you get the best balance for a sweet-spot experience.

MANAGING BODY SYMPTOMS

One of the easiest and most practical ways to dampen down nervous system activation is through some simple breathing and muscle-tension release exercises. These exercises have a good research evidence base outside of climbing,[3] and I have adapted them to be more specifically relevant to climbing so they can be used both on and off the rock.

a. **Breathing**

Breathing techniques can help with counteracting breath holding or breathing too fast, and can also be used just before and after a crux or series of delicate or dynamic moves. It's not realistic to keep your breathing slow and steady at all times, but rather once you have the hang of the breathing techniques off the rock, practise checking in with your breathing at regular intervals through your climb, for example, after every clip, during rests or every few moves. Relaxed breathing comes from our diaphragm, and has a slow steady out breath, with relaxed face and lips. This in turn is associated with less sympathetic nervous system activation (the nervous system associated with fight and flight) and more parasympathetic nervous system[4] action (the so-called rest and digest system). In my view, the way our body moves when we climb makes it more likely that we breathe from our chest rather than our belly (lots of shoulder involvement, core tension and delicate or dynamic moves, plus concentrating makes us do funny things with our breath!), and so making a conscious effort to breathe from your belly is important to counteract this. Often when we are stressed we are told to 'take a deep breath', but unfortunately following this advice tends to activate chest breathing rather than belly breathing. So instead, if you hear that phrase, try to think 'breathe out', and use a longer slower out breath as the start of a diaphragmatic breathing cycle. The exercise below is freely available as an audio download on my website.

Exercise 2: Breathing

It's easiest to start breathing practice by lying down, with one hand on your chest and one on your belly. Breathe normally for a few minutes – what do you notice? Our more relaxed breathing tends to come from the belly, with our belly hand rising as we breathe in, and falling as we breathe out. Next try a deep breath – which hand moves the most? Allow your breathing to settle back into coming more from the belly, using your diaphragm to move the air in and out of your lungs. As you breathe in, you can imagine a balloon expanding in your stomach, and as you breathe out, the balloon deflates. This is diaphragmatic breathing and is associated with being more relaxed.

Next, you can try to breathe out more slowly, making your out breath a little longer than your in breath. Try breathing in for the count of 3 and out for the count of 5, or in for 5 and out for 7. Finally, you can try to relax your face and lips as you breathe out, a technique I'm going to call 'horse lips' as you may make the sound of a horse as you breathe out! Breathing in this way is helpful for dampening down your nervous system arousal. When you have got this lying down, try the techniques standing up or walking around, before trying them whilst climbing.

Once you have mastered the art of breathing from your diaphragm, and generating a longer slower out breath, then it is important to practise the transition from either fast breathing or breath holding into more relaxed breathing. You might also want to practise whilst wearing a harness (think of pushing your belly out to fill your harness as you breathe in), and then on the wall or rock during easy moves, and on top rope before on lead. Once you have this dialled, you are ready to start trying the techniques out on harder stuff where you need to engage your core. Separating core tension from belly breathing is difficult, but it is possible with practice, and soon becomes second nature.

b. **Releasing muscle tension**

Climbing movements put a lot of tension through shoulders, neck and hands, areas which typically become tight in a situation where stress and anxiety are present. So we can think of climbing movements as perhaps increasing the likelihood for us to feel anxious through their effects on the body, when coupled with other triggers for anxiety such as tenuous moves or exposure. Anxiety tends also to lead to over-gripping, quickly causing a build-up of lactic acid in the forearms, and, of course, excess muscle tension through the body is also tiring. So learning to release any excess muscle tension from the body not only helps with physical fatigue but can also help to dissipate feelings of anxiety. Actions which lengthen and relax the muscles are again associated with parasympathetic nervous system activity, so helping to dampen down the fight-flight-freeze response.

The exercise below has been adapted from one used for decades as part of training a relaxation response outside of climbing; for me it also has the added benefit of helping to become more aware of different parts of the body and how and where tension is held and released. Body awareness and the ability to keep certain muscles tense (for example your core), whilst simultaneously relaxing other areas, is a helpful skill for movement efficiency, and if it also helps to reduce anxiety, what's not to like?

Exercise 3: Muscle release

Start by lying down in a comfortable position. You are going to tense and release each group of muscles in turn, breathing out as you release the tension. Start with your feet, and scrunch them up in your socks and shoes. Make the muscles as tight as you can, hold for a few seconds, then release and let them go floppy. Next, tighten all the muscles in your legs – thighs, calves, knees – all tight, hold for a few seconds, then release and let them go floppy. Now we are going to tighten your core muscles – belly, buttocks, back – all as tight as you can. Hold for a few seconds, then release. Next, let's tighten your arms, shoulders and hands – make fists, curl your biceps and bring your shoulders up to your ears. Hold for a few seconds, then release and let them all go floppy. Finally we are going to tense your head, face and neck. Tighten all the muscles in your jaw, bring your tongue to the roof of your mouth, scrunch up your face – make everything as tight as possible. Hold for a few seconds, then release and let your whole face relax. Now bring your whole body to a single point of tension – feet, legs, core, arms, face, all tight as you can. Hold it for a few seconds, then release and let all those muscles go floppy as you feel the tension draining away. Can you notice the difference?

Once you have mastered the long version, you can try a shorter version, just focusing on the shoulders, arms and face, tensing and releasing them together. This shorter version is really useful when you are belaying, or on a rest point, as a way of releasing excess muscle tension and preventing the build-up of stress in the body.

MANAGING FEELINGS

Wouldn't it be great if we could just stop feeling anxiety, fear, panic and other unpleasant emotions? This section title is a bit of a misnomer actually, as we have very little ability to manage our actual feelings, and we certainly can't get rid of them! Feelings or emotions are part of what makes us human; and having a range of different emotions is vital to human functioning. So trying to stop having feelings is futile; even so-called negative emotions like fear, anger and jealousy have a role in the human psyche, and are generally designed to help us stay in the social group, keep us safe and drive us towards resources for survival. Of course some are hugely powerful and all-consuming – what would be the point of them otherwise? They are designed to get us to act quickly, pushing out rational thought.

When we talk about managing our feelings, we are really talking about learning how to manage the behaviours which arise from our feelings. For example, if we feel angry, then it's more socially acceptable to express our anger in an assertive and calm way, than to shout and scream and punch the walls. Problems tend to arise when we fuse with our feelings; that is when we see our feelings as being a real 'thing' and allowing it to drive all our behaviour, rather than a set of body sensations, thoughts and behaviours which arise in relation to a particular circumstance. We can choose whether we allow our feelings to drive our behaviour (fused), or whether to ride them out and keep going in our valued direction.

In both ACT and mindfulness, feelings are viewed as something to be acknowledged and observed – they have useful data, but they don't last forever and will eventually pass. Cultivating this observer position is similar to that used with thoughts; we ground ourselves and unhook, and then refocus on something helpful to climbing.

Exercise 4: I'm having a feeling...

Learning to label the feelings we have can be helpful in giving a little space between us and the feeling itself. This is the observer position in action – there is a core 'you' who can notice and observe your feelings, without getting too swept up in the them. Try saying 'I'm having a feeling of panic' or 'I'm noticing I'm having a feeling of fear', when those emotions arise when you are climbing. Ideally say them out loud, or even sing them to a familiar tune! This will help to create a little distance between you and the feeling, and you can watch it rise and fall in intensity.

You can adapt the above exercise using whatever words feel good to you; for example, you could say 'here's panic again!' or 'hello scary feelings' – whatever works for you. The key here is to notice and acknowledge the feeling, and to externalise it by naming it as something *happening* to you ('I've got some nervous feelings happening'), rather than something you *are* ('I am nervous').

MANAGING FEARFUL AND NEGATIVE THOUGHTS ON THE ROCK

When we are feeling nervous, our internal chatter can get very loud, very negative and feel quite overwhelming. It can be hard to remember, in that moment, that our thoughts are just electrical impulses whizzing between our brain cells – they may feel real, powerful and tangible, but they are just made up of words and images created by our brain. Our thoughts might be about things which haven't yet happened like 'I'm going to fall' (but haven't done so yet!); 'I'm getting pumped' (yet still hanging on); or relate to events in the past 'why do I always get so scared?'; 'last time I led I was terrified and it was so embarrassing'. Ideally, we would want our thoughts to be about what will help us climb, rather than dwelling on past mistakes or future imaginings.

a. **Just thoughts**

The first thing to understand is that our thoughts are just thoughts, no matter how powerful they seem in the moment. They are just words and images in our minds, conjured up by neurons firing in our brain. They are usually about things which haven't yet happened, or which have happened in the past ('you're going to fall' or 'why do I always get scared?!'). Paying too much attention to them is not going to help you climb better at this point. Instead, we need to dissolve them back into just letters and sounds.

Exercise – Milk

Try saying the word 'milk' out loud. Notice what happens – do you get an image in your mind of a glass of milk? A carton of oat milk? Do you think about the taste or having it in your tea? Do you think about making pancakes with milk, or do images of cows pop up? Notice how many associated thoughts you get as you think about milk and where your mind takes you. Now try saying the word 'milk' over and over again. What happens now? Try it faster and faster or in a funny voice. What happens now? What happens to those associated thoughts and images? Do they begin to dissolve into just a noise?

You can try a version of this as you are climbing. Try saying any thoughts you have out loud, very fast, or singing them or saying in a funny way. You may feel a bit silly doing it, but if it helps you to dissolve the stranglehold your anxious thoughts have on you, then you will feel the benefit in your climbing.

b. Managing negative thoughts whilst actually climbing

I think sometimes there can be some confusion amongst climbers about how to manage negative thoughts. Ideas from cognitive behavioural therapy (CBT),[5] an approach which involves identifying and challenging negative thinking patterns, have filtered down to a degree to climbers, and often climbing clients I work with have tried to counteract their negative thoughts with more positive ones. For example, if you have the thought 'I'm going to fall', then climbers might say, 'my gear is good'. However, if you have actually tried this, you'll know that all the positive affirmations can sound a little hollow when you are 10 feet above the last piece of gear and you can't see any decent holds ahead! It is also a misunderstanding of the principles of CBT, which is not to try to replace negative thoughts with positive ones, but, rather, to introduce *cognitive doubt* to ideas which seem at the time to be unshakeable. Furthermore, we want our focus to be on finding holds, sequences and clipping positions – things that will help us climb – rather than getting wrapped up in a mental argument. CBT techniques can be helpful, but in my experience, they are more helpful off the rock than on it.

So, I'm going to distinguish here between techniques you can use whilst actually climbing, and those that are more helpful when you have finished your route or problem, and have time to sit down with a pen and paper and analyse what happened. On the rock, we are going to use techniques from an approach called acceptance and commitment therapy (ACT);[6] a newer type of cognitive therapy with a good evidence base, and from mindfulness,[7] which is often used in ACT. Mindfulness has in fact been around for centuries, as a way of being present in the here and now. If you are interested in mindfulness, then the book *Wherever You Go, There You Are*, by Jon Kabat Zinn, is a good introduction.

In ACT we talk about getting hooked by unhelpful thoughts and feelings, which I think conveys the power of our thoughts. We get hooked and act as if they were real, tangible and manifesting right here and now. Learning how to unhook from those thoughts and keep our focus on valued actions is a good way to shift your focus from the what-ifs to the what-to-dos. You'll remember from chapter 2 that we spent some time figuring out what our life and climbing values are; now is the time to unhook from thoughts which move us away from those values. For example, if I have the thought that I'm going to fall, and I can unhook from this thought, then I am more likely to keep trying hard to send my route, moving towards my climbing values. For more details about ACT, check out *ACT in Sport*[8] by James Hegarty and Christoph Huelsmann.

Exercise 5: Unhooking from thoughts[9]

One of the easiest ways to unhook from thoughts, which also goes well with breathing from the belly, is to sing your thoughts out loud to a tune like Happy Birthday *or* The Sun Has Got His Hat On *(or any other tune you know well). Using a technique like this, we create a little distance between our self and thoughts, and this makes them a little less all-consuming. You could also try saying the thoughts out loud using different voices, such as very high– or low-pitched, or like your favourite actor, or with a really posh accent. This often allows you to see them for what they are – just a collection of words, letters and sounds made up by our brain.*

Sometimes the thoughts can be so powerful, loud and overwhelming, it's just too difficult to unhook straight away. In those instances, we might need to use a grounding technique to get out of our minds and back into our bodies and the present. Grounding techniques usually use a sensory focus to bring the mind back to the here and now. They can help with unhooking from thoughts and are often used with people who experience panic or even dissociative experiences due to trauma. Many grounding exercises have their roots in a practice called mindfulness. Mindfulness is defined as paying attention to the here and now, without judgement. You can find mindfulness through formal meditation practices, but it is also an attitude or way of being, observing your inner world with curiosity and openness. If you practise mindfulness therefore, it can have benefits in terms of allowing you to ride out negative thoughts, observing them but not getting caught up in them, as well as increasing your awareness of the sensory experience of climbing. However, it's not for everyone, and should be used cautiously if you have severe trauma or experiences of hearing voices – if that's you, then do seek advice from a qualified practitioner first.

There are many different mindfulness exercises to try, but for climbers, using those which can have a functional impact on climbing is most appropriate. These include mindfulness of breathing, and a technique called the Soles of the Feet[10] (adapted from Singh et al., 2008), to shift the focus onto the feet, always helpful in climbing!

Exercise 6: Soles of the feet

Standing up, close your eyes if you feel comfortable, and bring you awareness down into your right foot, and into your right big toe. Just try to notice any sensations you feel there. Heat, cold, pain perhaps, the shape and weight of your toe, anything at all. Try to give it all your focus for a moment. Then breathe out, and let it go. Move your awareness to your second toe. What can you notice here? Whatever you feel, it's ok, and if you notice nothing at all, that's also ok. Try to be open to noticing whatever is there. And if your attention wanders, then gently bring it back to your second toe. Then breathe out, and let it go. Next bring your awareness to your third toe. What do you notice here? The shape and weight, any sensations, where your toe touches your sock or your shoe, or the floor perhaps. Try to keep your awareness on your third toe. Then breathe out, and let it go. Now bring your awareness to your fourth toe. This one might be harder to find, but just see what you can notice here. Can you feel its shape? And if you feel nothing at all, that is also fine, just stay with feeling nothing. Then breathe out and let it go. Now your little toe. What can you notice here? Become aware of the shape, weight, any sensations of cold, heat, pain or just which parts touch your sock or shoe or the floor. Then breathe out and let it go. Now bring your awareness to the ball of your foot, that big pad of flesh. Feel the shape and weight of it. Feel the areas which touch the floor and those which do not. What other sensations can you notice? Can you feel the floor underneath, pushing back up at the ball of your foot? Then breathe out and let it go. Now the heel, what can you notice about your heel? Can you feel the shape of your heel, any points of pressure or contact with the floor? Where does your weight lie? Can you feel the sensation of the floor underneath, supporting your heel? Now breathe out and let it go. Finally, try to feel your foot as a whole – the toes, the ball of the foot and the heel. Feel the points of contact with the floor and the floor underneath, supporting your whole foot. Keep your awareness of your whole foot for a moment. Now breathe out and let it go. What do you notice now about your right foot, and your left foot? Now repeat the exercise with your left foot.

I really like this exercise, as it helps to really connect with our feet, and with footwork being so important for climbing, I feel it is a great way to get out of our tangled thoughts and back into our bodies, ready for climbing. Again, this needs practice to be really useful, but you can do this whole exercise before starting a route or problem, and once you are well practised, a shorter version will work where you just take your awareness into your whole foot, perhaps on a rest, at a stance, or when resting between attempts.

Once we have grounded ourselves and got back in the present, and started to unhook from negative thoughts, then it is time to shift our focus back to climbing-relevant stimuli. When we get nervous, our hold search strategy tends to become less efficient, we may overgrip and lean in more, and both of these effects can lead to a decreased ability to see holds and sequences. Using an active strategy to focus fully on the rock can be helpful at this point. Focusing strategies are discussed more fully in section 3.

c. **What not to do with thoughts**

You may see in some older sport psychology books or articles a technique called 'thought stopping' for negative thoughts.[11] This can be carried out in several ways, but it involves actively trying to stop thoughts by either saying 'stop' out loud or in your mind. You may also see this paired with twanging an elastic band on your wrist every time you have the thought. I absolutely do NOT recommend you use this technique, since it has been shown to increase rather than decrease negative thoughts.[12] This technique was previously used for people with intrusive thoughts (often as part of a condition called obsessive compulsive disorder, or OCD), but recent research has found that it actually results in a rebound effect,[13] whereby even if you get a temporary reduction in negative thoughts, they tend to come back later on with renewed vigour. Indeed, one of the key maintaining factors for all anxiety conditions is that the person's attempts to not think about difficult thoughts, whether mentally trying to stop them or through rituals and compulsions designed to neutralise them, tends to reinforce and increase the thoughts rather than stopping them.

d. **Dealing with negative thoughts and core beliefs off the rock**

After your climbing session is where more well-known CBT techniques can be useful. Remember, CBT is not about thinking positively or developing some mantras or affirmations. Cognitive behavioural techniques help you to introduce doubt to ideas and thoughts which seem at the time to be absolute. Keeping a thought record as discussed in chapter 4 will allow you to see patterns of negative thoughts, and help you to determine whether they came true or not. What was the evidence for that particular thought? What other thoughts were linked to that negative thought – what was the thought cascade? How much did you believe each thought at the time? How accurate was that thought? What did you do as a result of that thought cascade and what impact did that have? When you have some of these answers written down, you can start to move onto challenging your negative thoughts and introducing doubt. This will allow you to unhook from these thoughts more quickly next time you are in a stressful climbing situation. There is an example of a thought record below, with columns to help you to introduce doubt to your negative thinking patterns.

Situation	Negative thought	How much do you believe the negative thought? How likely is it to happen 0–100%	Evidence for the negative thought	Evidence against the negative thought	Alternative thoughts and explanations	How much do you believe the negative thought now? How likely is it to happen 0–100%
Example: Above my bolt, next move looks reachy	'I can't reach that'	75%	I'm only 5'4"	It's within my grade so there is probably a solution	I need to find a good sequence	50%
	'I'm going to fall'	90%	I don't climb dynamically	I haven't fallen yet and I've got lots of stamina so I can take time to work it out	If I get my feet up, I'll be ok	30%
	'It's embarrassing that I can't even climb a F5+'	100%	I'm feeling shaky I hate crying when I'm climbing	No-one is really watching apart from my partner	Falling off means I'm trying hard and that's good	10%

As you can see above, all that we need to do is introduce some doubt to our negative thoughts, rather than replacing them with positive ones. Weakening our certainty in the negatives helps by improving our willingness and commitment to having a go, *despite* feeling anxious.

Our negative thought patterns can also give clues as to our underlying beliefs and assumptions, as discussed in chapter 4. Using a technique called the downward arrow technique (discussed later), we can get at some of the assumptions that we hold and determine whether these are accurate or not, helpful or unhelpful, or whether they are as important as they once were or no longer relevant. Core beliefs usually centre around ourselves, the world and other people, and can determine how we think, feel and behave, in a kind of 'unwritten rule' type way. They are the lens through which we see the world and were often developed when we were quite young, or through some key experiences. Exercises for challenging unhelpful core beliefs are discussed later in this book, but there is an example below which helps to illustrate their impact.

Climber study: Cora

Cora was finding her lead climbing at a standstill despite having really good technique when she bouldered or seconded. Some of the negative thoughts she was having included things like 'I'm taking too long' and 'I'm not good enough to lead this'. Using the downward arrow technique, we discovered that Cora had some beliefs about how a good lead climber should be – they must always be fast, efficient and never make mistakes. She had some old beliefs about mistakes always being bad, embarrassing and meaning she was incompetent. These core beliefs were piling on the pressure when Cora wanted to lead, making her rush the preparation and the route, and failing to course-correct when she made a misstep. This was leading to crushing embarrassment and reinforced the idea that she was not good enough to lead. When we tackled these core beliefs, Cora found that she was able to dismiss some of the negative thoughts, and climb in a way which suited her better.

Climbers are often surprised when they unpick their core beliefs and figure out some of the assumptions they hold can be looked at in a different way. Remember, the idea is not to convince ourselves of the opposite – so in Cora's case, we were not trying to convince her that she was a quick climber or good enough to lead. We were simply aiming to *introduce doubt* to those strongly held beliefs, and in doing so open up a space for new possibilities. So for Cora, we opened up the space that a good climber could take their time, and that mistakes could be useful for learning.

MANAGING FEAR BEHAVIOURS

As a general principle, whatever fear behaviours you have, you will need to try to do the opposite. If you are not sure what you do, then your belayer or regular climbing partner will probably have a good idea! So, if you tend to rush when scared, then slow down and try to move in a tai-chi style, with no sudden movements, just slow and steady but continuous movement. If you become combative and fight your way up the route, then consciously relax your muscles and try not to swear; you could also try softening your gaze, or even singing something softer and romantic! If you tend to freeze up, then work on creating small movements by staying on the holds but swaying a little side to side or up onto your toes a little and back down. You can then work up to taking a foot off, next maybe up an inch and back down, before gradually working up to committing to the move. The important thing is to practise these ideas in a low-stress situation, then practise transitioning from your usual fight-flight-freeze pattern into the opposite, before trying them out for real on the rock.

MANAGING SAFETY-SEEKING BEHAVIOURS

You'll recall from chapter 4 that you filled out a list of psychological safety–seeking behaviours. These are things we do which make us feel safer (though they make very little real difference to our safety) but keep us stuck in the anxiety cycle. If these habits are very ingrained then you are going to need to wean yourself off them slowly. Start by putting them in order of the easiest to deal with to the hardest, and then practise removing them in low-stress situations first (for example with a belayer you trust and in the gym rather than at the top of Dinas Cromlech!). With behaviours which are habitual like knot checking, it can be helpful to have your belayer count how many times you check your knot normally, and then gradually reduce from there, perhaps planning to check only at each clip, and then every other clip, and then every third clip and so on. Any time you are removing psychological safety behaviours, try to do this with relaxed breathing and relaxed muscles, so you begin to associate these times with a more relaxed body physiology. Remember, you still want to do buddy checks and have good communication on the ground – this is 'real' safety behaviour – but you want to remove *psychological* safety–seeking behaviours which serve to maintain anxiety.

MANAGING AVOIDANCE

Long term, it pays to work on your weaknesses and start to tackle all the types of rock, routes and moves that you would typically avoid. You might choose big projects which are your preferred style of climbing, but for training purposes, killing avoidance makes a lot of sense. By trying slopey hold climbs, or corners or getting on grit cracks, you learn to broaden your climbing repertoire and build a bigger bank of experiences. But it is important again that it is done in the right way and not too overwhelming, or you will simply solidify in your mind that hand jamming (for example) is terrifying. It's important to recognise the mental element of this exercise, and so dial back the risk of becoming anxious by dialling down the difficulty, and dialling up the protection (for example practising on top rope or isolating a move low down above a bouldering mat).

Spend some time analysing what you tend to avoid when climbing by thinking about the physical elements you avoid (style of climbing, rock type, moves), the social elements you avoid (climbing in busy gyms for example, or climbing somewhere isolated perhaps), and the interpersonal elements you avoid (climbing with new belayers or climbers who climb a lot harder than you). Develop a hierarchy from least to most scary to tackle, and, then, start to work your way through them slowly, remembering to use your relaxed breathing and muscles, and grounding techniques as you go. This is not a quick exercise so don't expect to whip through the hierarchy in one go; you'll need to practise regularly to undo avoidance, particularly if it's long-term avoidance. Of course, the biggest avoidance for most people is around climbing to the point of failure, particularly when lead climbing. Commonly referred to as a fear of falling, in the next chapter we'll identify that a fear of falling can often be due to multiple fears, and then figure out the best way to tackle the various fears which can inhibit climbers from climbing to point of failure. There is more detail on working through a fear hierarchy in chapter 8, where you can simply substitute exposing yourself to falling, for anything else you may be avoiding.

MANAGING A PANIC ATTACK

If anxiety levels build too much, then a panic attack becomes likely. This is quite a dangerous situation for lead climbers, in that the desire to get out of there can push people to start rushing up the crag and in their haste be more likely to take a bad fall, or become crag-fast and need rescue skills from their belayer. Some of you reading this book will have experienced this, and will also know that a panic attack at the crag is a terrifying experience and likely to destroy any leading confidence you have.

If you do find yourself building towards a panic attack, try to clip into gear or put more gear in. If you can hang in your harness then do so, but above all, try to stay put for a while. A panic attack will not last for ever, though it will feel like it is at the time.

During a panic attack, we tend to hyperventilate, our heart rate shoots up and we can feel dizzy or even have a sense of impending doom or death. Not pleasant at all and likely to drive out any rational thought! This is where your belayer comes in, in that if they can see and hear you, they can prompt you to take action to bring the panic under control again. You are not likely to be thinking for yourself, and survival behaviours can take over. A well-prepared belayer can remind you of ways to manage that panic, so if this is something that affects you, do discuss with your belayer what they can do to help.

Managing your breathing is likely to be the most effective, but no one carries a paper bag up a route! This is the traditional method of sorting out your breathing during a panic attack, which helps to manage levels of carbon dioxide – we need a certain amount of carbon dioxide to cue our lungs to breathe in again, and hyperventilating can flush out too much CO_2 and lead to increasingly effortful breathing, compounding the panic. If you are wearing a loose top, you can tuck your head into it to simulate breathing into a paper bag. If not, and you can, then cupping your hands and breathing into them is another option. If none of these is available to you, then simply focusing on slowing your out breath down will help, as if blowing bubbles under water. Eventually the feelings of panic will subside, but you are going to feel quite shaky for a while, and so if possible I would advise staying put and getting someone to throw you a rope, or building a belay and bringing up your second, or simply lowering off and leaving your gear. Climbers are generally a community-minded bunch, and crag swag often gets returned via climbing forums or Facebook groups.

SUMMARY

Practise the skills of managing nerves, stress and anxiety regularly off the wall/rock, at the foot of the crag, at the top of the crag and in the climbing wall, before expecting to be able to use them whilst climbing. Once you have them down, then it's time to start using them as part of your climbing tool kit, and they should be as vital and well known to you as your rack. Also crucial is using the skills soon enough, and not waiting for a full-blown panic before starting your breathing or muscle relaxation. The sooner you employ them, the more likely you are to keep your anxiety levels manageable and prevent an all out panic. It is better to lower off, rather than drive yourself into a panic attack, since the impact on your confidence is going to be fairly catastrophic and last a long time. Discretion really is the better part of valour – remember that if anxiety has dogged your climbing career, you are better off aiming to slightly fall short of that arousal-performance sweet spot, than to get over-psyched and fall off the performance cliff. As you start to become more successful in managing your nerves, then your confidence will grow and you can increase the challenge gradually. Learning to tolerate anxiety takes time, so practising these skills should not be rushed. Remember to mix in plenty of lower-challenge routes or problems to give yourself some success in between.

CHAPTER 6

Fear of falling – what to consider

Falling practice has been a mainstay of any book, article or coaching practice for climbers who have worries and fears about falling when lead climbing. And yet, for me now, it is rarely the 'go to' exercise, for many reasons. First, for many climbers, falling practice is extremely aversive, and for that reason, may make their fear worse not better. If you find falling off really horrible, then you are unlikely to be able to carry out the practice often enough, for long enough and in a relaxed enough way, to really get used to it and not inadvertently increase your fear rather than decreasing it. Second, falling practice assumes that the only scary bit of falling is the sensation of dropping onto the rope, whereas for many people, they are plagued by images of cams ripping out, their knot undoing, their belayer not catching them, and multiple other ways of plummeting to the floor. There is a huge element of trust involved in belayer, rope, gear and the whole system, which often needs to be tackled in its own right, rather than indirectly via taking a fall. Third, some climbers have had very negative or even traumatic experiences of falling in the past, and for them, the worst thing to do is to initiate falling practice without a thorough assessment first, because this can simply be re-traumatising.

I also wonder whether we have been putting the emphasis on the wrong part of falling. Climbing is an unusual sport in practising falling

– most other sports where falling might occur will practise committing to trying really hard even if falling is a possibility, rather than practising a fall itself. For example, gymnasts never practise falling off the beam or bars, though they do practise landing. Horse riders never practise falling off at a jump, but they do practise committing to riding forwards despite the possibility of a stop and a fall. It's rare to practise what we don't want to see, simply because we don't want to reinforce that occurring. What if emphasising the fall was the wrong thing to concentrate on? How might we alter our practice if we focused instead on trying really hard and committing to moves, despite the possibility of falling, or if we focused on landing really well? This would certainly give a different flavour to the practice; it may also prevent that time honoured way of getting out of an unexpected fall – taking a premature jump off the rock, before the rock spits you off.

WHAT'S INVOLVED IN FEELING COMFORTABLE TO FALL?

I haven't yet seen any research which maps out all the elements you need in place to feel comfortable with taking a fall, but below you will see my own map of the factors I consider when coaching someone with a fear of falling. You can use this map to think about your own worries about falling, and score each element on a scale of 0–10, in terms of how comfortable you feel with each component (with 10 being super-confident). Mapping it out in this way will give you a guide as to what you need to tackle, and in what order of importance (Figure 6.1).

Some of the elements below are covered in my Fear of Falling Workbook, *which is a practical resource companion designed to take you step by step through taking fall practice. The broader skills such as tactics, flow and motivation are also covered in this book.*

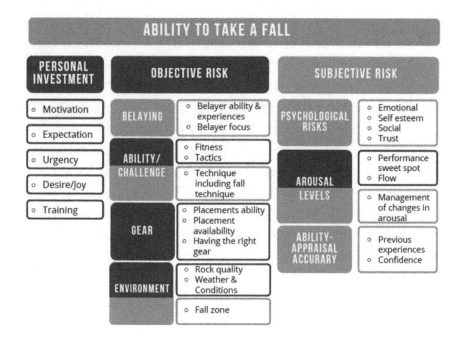

FIGURE 6.1 *Ability to Take a Fall Chart, Retrieved from Williams (2021).*

Broadly, our ability to handle a fall can be split into our desire for the route itself, and how much that outweighs any worry or fear; the elements which make up the objective risks of falling; and those which make up the perceived risks of falling. Whilst many of the psychological elements increase or decrease the sense of perceived risk, there are also key components which alter the objective risk for the climber which have a psychological slant. For example, the relationship with the belayer is a crucial part of feeling safe to fall, and this cannot be ignored if you want to get on top of a fear of falling.

TRUST

Trust is central to the ability to take a fall in pursuit of a lead. We need to trust the gear, the rock, the rope, the belay device and the belayer. We need to trust ourselves to land correctly, and we need to feel an element of trust with respect to managing our own emotions and how we are perceived by those around us. For example, if I feel embarrassed about screaming as I fall, then this is going to inhibit my sense of relaxation about falling. In my view, this component of falling is often neglected and assumed to be in place. However, if you have never weighted your gear, never allowed your belayer to catch an unexpected fall even on a top rope or respond quickly to any other unexpected event, then there can be many unknowns which can inhibit your sense of trust in the process. The first step therefore is, as always, an honest appraisal of the degree of trust you feel in each element of the system, and also in your regular belay partners. The self-assessments below will guide you as to what you might need to work on, with practical exercises to try out.

TRUST IN YOUR BELAYER

Use the assessment below to consider the level of trust you have in each of your regular belay partners.

Exercise: Assessing your level of trust in your belayer

Rate your belayer on each of the following on scale of 0–10, where 0 is terrible and 10 is perfect. Then make a note of why you have not scored them higher on this characteristic. What does this say about your belaying and climbing partnership? What can you and they do (it's a partnership right?) to increase the scores by 1?

1. *How much do you trust your belayer to catch you if you fall?*
2. *To what degree do you feel an equal partner in the relationship?*
3. *Who chooses where you go and the routes?*
4. *How supportive is your belayer?*
5. *How motivating is your belayer?*
6. *Can you trust your belayer to get you out of trouble?*

7. *How much on the same wavelength are you both?*
8. *To what degree do you feel able to be vulnerable in front of your belayer?*
9. *Can you fully focus on your climbing or do you keep half an eye/ear on your belayer?*
10. *Does your belayer do anything else which helps or hinders your climbing? To what degree?*

You will probably find that you have more trust in some people than others, which is normal and natural. Trust is affected by things like length and quality of the relationship, thoughtfulness, communication and attunement (how 'in tune' you are with each other). Whilst for some relationships it will be easy to increase the level of trust through some simple exercises, it does very much depend on the person and their willingness to engage in discussions and exercises about trust, and you might feel that although some belay partners are fun to hang out with, you will never fully trust them to belay you when you are climbing at your limit. That is absolutely fine, and the key here is to recognise this, and decide who is your 'easy day' partner, and who is your 'pushing the boat out' partner. I would recommend that if you have someone where there is already a trusting relationship with good communication between you, that you talk to them about how to increase the level of trust between both of you so you can fine-tune the belaying to be as solid (practically and emotionally) as possible.

EXERCISES TO INCREASE TRUST IN YOUR PARTNER

If you are both open to increasing the trust in your relationship, then here are some ideas for how to do this off the wall, as well as on the wall. Your aim here is to have total faith in your belayer, so that once you have had your discussion and buddy checks on the ground, you have a strong sense of connection that doesn't need checking whilst you are climbing.

Exercises to increase trust[1]

Discuss

Talk to your belayer about how you both like to be belayed. Do you prefer it quiet, do you like encouragement, do you like or not like beta or route suggestions, do you prefer them to not chat to others, for example. Take 5 minutes each, and without interrupting the other person, tell each other about your belaying preferences. Then, the listening person can ask some questions to clarify any points. Try not to get defensive if you feel your belaying is being criticised, but to be open-minded to the learning points. If you've had bad belaying in the past, if you are worried about losing control and crying on a route, or you feel embarrassed that you don't even want to lead – whatever it is, these fears and shames tend to grow in the dark. Be brave and open up to your belayer because the very act of revealing your private fears shows a level of trust and will take away some of the secret shame attached to them. If you are listening to a big reveal, try to stay quiet, let the other person speak and listen wholeheartedly. Ask some questions, but try not to fix it for them. Ideally take turns to do this so it feels equal.

Trust exercises

Floor-based trust exercises like leaning back towards your belayer and letting them catch you can help, especially if you dislike being out of control. Try falling backwards into your belayer's arms, being led around blindfolded or even over a small obstacle course. Take turns and notice any thoughts or feelings which crop up for you. Can you allow yourself to fully trust your partner/belayer? Aim to stay relaxed in your breathing and body as you try these exercises.

Learn how to give a soft catch

Giving a soft catch can be difficult if you have never been shown how, and especially if you are anxious yourself. Book a coach to work with you both for an hour to help refine your technique, or find an experienced belayer who is used to belaying people redpointing or onsighting hard stuff and ask them to show you. If you are nervous of falling, then get someone who isn't scared to take the falls for you so you can practise catching. Knowing that you both can give a soft catch can help you feel more confident.

Good belaying

Do you pay attention when your partner is climbing? If your mind tends to wander, or you find yourself chatting to others when you're belaying, have you thought about the subconscious effect of this on your own climbing? By being distracted you may be creating a doubt in your own mind about whether belayers truly concentrate, not something you want for your own turn climbing. Practise being an attentive, but relaxed belayer, and you will be strengthening the association in your own mind between belaying and concentrating.

Fun

Try to have some fun together, particularly if your climbing partnership is mostly about training and sending. Try some climbing games together, some aerial dance on a rope, try speed climbing, goof around a bit trying to climb in a funny style – anything that breaks up the usual pattern. Knowing your belayer is there with you when you are climbing in unexpected ways can help to build a bank of good experiences.

Part of trusting your belayer is feeling psychologically safe in the partnership overall. Climbing partnerships sometimes run into trouble because they feel unequal in some way, and it's important to be mindful of who makes the decisions, how you 'encourage' each other, and whose needs have precedence in the partnership. The tendency can be to let the climber who climbs hardest take the lead in the decision making, but over time this can have a negative effect on the partnership. Even if you don't tend to lead, it is important for there to be a sense of balance. Have a think about the following questions.

1. How do you feel overall about your regular climbing partner and your partnership together?
2. What do you feel is important *for you* in a climbing partnership?
3. To what extent do you feel your climbing partner gives you what you need to climb at your best?
4. What annoying habits does your climbing partner have?
5. What things do they do which help your climbing?
6. What things do they do which do not help your climbing?
7. How well do you communicate together?
8. To what extent can you tell your climbing partner if you are feeling scared, embarrassed, angry, etc.
9. Does your climbing partnership feel equal and balanced?
10. Can you have fun with your climbing partner?

If both parties are willing to take part in improving the partnership, try to open up a discussion about what helps and hinders your climbing. If you need to ask your regular climbing partner to stop doing something, make sure your communication is clear and assertive. Assertive communication is not aggressive or confrontational, but does use clear 'I' statements, such as 'I feel', 'I need' and 'It helps me'. Do not blame the other person or use phrases such as 'you make me feel…' since this is likely to result in defensive responses and close down the discussion. Sometimes, it's simply that neither party has aired what they want and have made assumptions about being on the same page. We tend to see the world through the lens of our own experiences and beliefs, and your partner may have missed that you have a different take on things. So, tell your climbing partner what your climbing objectives are and how they can help you. Make sure that you also spend time listening to your climbing partner, and ask them questions about what they need from you. It's ok to have different objectives or ideals from a session, provided there is equal time for both of you to arrange to take turns in some way. Be honest about what you want and explicitly ask what the other person wants too; beware of being passive in the partnership and letting the other person always choose venues, routes and when you climb. Having a sense of agency is important for our self-confidence.

TRUST IN THE GEAR SYSTEMS

There are many components to the lead system – rope, quickdraws and extenders, gear, gear placements and the system as a whole. Whilst you may not know or even need to know how many kilonewtons a nut 5 holds, it is important for trust and confidence that you understand how they work and that you have tested out these elements of the system in a safe and controlled way. Otherwise, when you come close to lobbing off that thin HVS, you may find that you have a lot of question marks in your mind which will interfere with your ability to commit to the moves. Use the self-assessment below to score your understanding in and ability to trust the various parts of the system.

Exercise: Assessing your trust in climbing gear and catching/landing systems

Assess yourself on a scale of 0–10 on the following questions.

1. *I know how bolts are placed in the rock*
2. *I know how nuts work*
3. *I know how cams work*
4. *I know how hexes work*
5. *I understand how various belay devices work and which to use when*
6. *I know how to decide what length of quick draw to use*
7. *I know where to use pulley quick draws and where not to*
8. *I know how and when to use a 'cheat' quick draw and clip stick*

9. *I know how to work out where my fall zone is/how far I might fall*
10. *I know when to retire my gear and ropes*
11. *I know which type of rope to use when (single, double, thickness, etc.)*
12. *I know how to self-rescue in a variety of different situations*
13. *I know what to do after I have fallen on a piece of gear*
14. *I know how to get back on the rock after a fall if the route is overhanging*
15. *I know how and when to secure my belayer at the bottom of the route, or on a belay stance*
16. *I know how to think about the best place to stand when belaying*
17. *I know where to place a bouldering mat in relation to different angles of the rock*
18. *I know how to spot a boulderer depending on the direction of fall and ground level/obstacles*
19. *I know how best to use quick draws and krabs if I am working a sport route*
20. *I know what to do to minimise wear and tear on fixed anchors*
21. *I know how to set up a retrievable and fixed line abseil*
22. *I know how to set up a top rope outdoors*

Now that you have an idea of where you feel less trusting or perhaps have less understanding of how a particular element works, you can begin to prioritise your efforts. Order the elements above, from the lowest knowledge and trust scores, to the highest, and work your way up from the bottom. You might want to enlist the help of an MCI (or international equivalent) if you have knowledge gaps, but for trust gaps, it is usually possible to work on this yourself, with some help from a friend or two.

Commonly, climbers have rarely even sat on their gear, for example at a trad belay, tending to stand or lean in and not weight the gear so never resting fully into their harness. They might never have sat into their harness at the top of a sport climb until their belayer has them pulled in tight. They may never have seen a bolt being placed, and perhaps have no trust that it is firmly anchored to the wall. It is possible to work on all these elements, but the key here is it must be done in a manageable way, with good relaxation at every stage, so that lowering onto the gear does not become a tense and worrisome experience, for example. Use the skills you have learnt in chapter 5 whilst working on any trust gaps.

OTHER SOURCES OF ANXIETY IN THE CLIMBER–BELAYER RELATIONSHIP: BELAYING ITSELF

Whilst it's easy to see how your level of trust in your belayer and the gear and systems can impact on the stress of climbing, what may not be so apparent is the impact of the stress associated with belaying your climbing partner on your own climbing. Belaying another climber is a huge responsibility, and this sense of responsibility may be increased when it is your life partner you are belaying, or the climber is trying a route at their limit, or perhaps if your experience levels don't broadly match up, or even if your body weights do not tally. If we are belaying well, then we are vigilant, watchful, ready to respond in an instant – we are on high alert, and unfortunately this is a quality associated with a heightened stress response.

We may not have had much experience at catching falls, or be worried about what to do if the climber falls off on the overhanging section and how to help them get back on the route. We may be calculating whether to jump off our own belay ledge if they fall in order to lessen the length or impact of fall for them, or what to do if they have a really bad fall and hit their heads. Running through a host of 'what if' scenarios gives us some cognitive presses for an increased arousal level or stress response.

Finally, the body position we hold when belaying may also feed our anxiety. We may find that we grip the rope, stand with our head back looking up so pinching our neck, shoulders up, tense in our lower body ready to brace for a fall. These are all body indicators of increased arousal and stress, and when we take these changes in body tension, cognitive arousal and behaviour, we can see that we are beginning to feed the anxiety cycle we discussed in chapter 4.

So if we spend some time on high alert or even stressed whilst belaying, what impact does this have on our own climbing? More often than not, climbers take little time to bring their own anxiety levels down before setting off on their own climb. They are then starting with a heightened level of arousal, and this means that they are more likely to tip over into anxiety more quickly than they might have done if they had not had a stressful belaying experience. It is crucial to recognise the impact of belaying on your own internal arousal levels, and to take the time to mitigate for this before starting your own climb.

Climber study: Gina

Gina climbed at roughly the same level as her partner, but there was a substantial weight difference between them – not enough to make a big deal out of it, but enough that Gina would spend much of the route praying that Riley did not fall off whilst at the same time being outwardly encouraging and supportive. Riley also tended to speed up later on in the route and sometimes made some lunging moves, and Gina would be braced for these moves and ready to manage the rope in case of a fall. They always had limited time to climb, and so Gina would just jump straight onto her route, but often found that her leading was affected by anxiety.

Gina wasn't keen to talk to Riley about her worries as she didn't want to impact on their climbing confidence. Instead, we worked on using belly breathing and shoulder muscle tense and release for when

she was belaying, alongside belay glasses to improve her neck posi-
tion. We also spent some time looking at the pros and cons of their
current pattern and rhythm of swinging the lead. Riley tended to like
to go first and Gina liked a warm-up whilst seconding, but she agreed
to experiment with other ways of warming up (such as bouldering at
the foot of the crag), and taking turns to only lead or only second on
that day. Gina also worked on figuring out how to bring her anxiety
levels down after belaying Riley, and only getting on her climb when
she felt calm enough to do so and there wasn't any adrenalin still
washing round her body. We felt that fewer climbs in a more relaxed
state were better than more climbs with higher stress for her long-
term development and confidence.

CONTINGENCY PLANS

There is a lot of 'think positive' advice out there which can sometimes
lead climbers to think that it is better not to think about what might go
wrong on a climb. Some climbers may even feel a sense of superstition
about preparing for the worst, but thinking about all the 'what-ifs' *in*
advance (that bit is crucial!) is not going to make them happen. Indeed,
thinking about all possible outcomes and preparing a plan for how to
deal with them can give a sense of confidence and allow them to be put
to bed mentally, knowing that if the time comes, you will know what to
do. We will cover this in terms of visualisation in section 3, but it is also
worthwhile making some written plans and even practising potential
scenarios in real life if you can. The military take this to an extreme,
constantly drilling and practising various scenarios so their personnel
can operate almost automatically if the worst happens, and we can
certainly learn some lessons from this approach.

So, if you find leading stressful, or are planning to push the boat out with
a climb that is a stretch for you, it is worth borrowing some military tac-

tics and figuring out where the gaps in your knowledge are (do you need to get some advice on how to prusik up a rope for example?); where the possible sticking points of the route are; and what your escape options are. For example, if you know the crux is a bit marginal for you, can you put some extra gear in below so you can hang out there if needed whilst you figure out your strategy, or if you should take a fall? Or in the event you don't feel able to continue, then do you have an older krab and sling you don't mind leaving behind so you can lower off? You can also use the contents of your anxious thoughts when climbing to help you to figure out what is worrying you and how you can prepare for it. Remember, anxiety tends to push us to avoid thinking about scenarios that cause us anxiety, and by acknowledging these fears and worries and coming up with a plan for these possible future scenarios, we are beginning to tackle the avoidance. This will have a positive effect on anxiety levels. Be thorough, and brainstorm with your belay partner all the possible scenarios, and consider writing down your plan so you are clear in your mind and you each know exactly what to do. This will allow you to then mentally 'park' the what-ifs and focus on your climbing.

ACCURATELY ASSESSING RISK

One of the big questions climbers often ask is, why am I so scared of falling when I know that it is relatively safe? The answer is that fear and perception of risk are not necessarily based on logic and current/absolute knowledge. Our first reflex fears as a baby and young child are of falling (those of you with children will have seen the Morrow reflex in action, where a baby automatically fans out its limbs then reflexively clutches in if you tilt its head downwards quickly. This is likely designed to slow and break a fall and then cling on) and of heights (which appears once babies start to crawl – experiments show babies unwilling to crawl across a glass floor with a drop underneath). These fears are hardwired into us to keep us safe, much like some of the common subjects of phobias such as spiders, snakes and other potentially poisonous creatures. Some people have these hardwired responses more strongly than others, possibly due to our ancestors' evolutionary journeys. Being at height and safe falls when climbing are therefore not necessarily neutral activities, but come with a strong pre-wired aversive response, kicking us quickly into the fight-flight-freeze response so we stay out of trouble. So many of us are having to work against thousands of years of evolution and learn to retrain our brain to feel comfortable with 'safe' falls.

We are also extremely motivated to avoid unpleasant emotions, and falling can trigger a range of responses. From fear itself, to a fear of fear, to embarrassment and shame at our behaviour when scared – there is a layering of emotions amplifying the unpleasantness, and leaving us determined to avoid similar situations in the future. Our ability to learn from unpleasant situations has been crucial to our survival, and so knowingly putting ourselves into situations where we have previously had horrible, overwhelming feelings, takes a lot of bravery, practice and skill.

So assessing risk is more complex than just judging the objective and physical characteristics of the situation; there are the emotional, social and psychological elements to consider. Whilst I'm not going to talk in detail about fall factors, gear strength and so on, it is important for climbers to be able to carry out a basic risk assessment before undertaking any fall practice, and also before leading. Bear in mind that certain psychological factors tend to alter your perception of risk, often without us realising. For example, being tired can negatively impact decision making[2] and lead to higher-risk strategies; being somewhere familiar may lead to underestimating risk,[3] and we may overestimate risk when we feel a lack of trust in the people with us. Having a checklist can be a useful way of making sure we have covered all the areas we need to factor in without taking mental shortcuts, and these will include a mix of relatively objective risks such as potential height of fall and rope stretch, alongside more personal and subjective factors such as grade confidence, physical and mental state and sense of familiarity.

If we are wanting to increase our confidence for a big lead, then we can manipulate these psychological factors to our advantage, for example, by becoming intimately familiar with a venue prior to going for a limit lead, but we should always bear in mind that this will only alter the subjective risks and not the objective ones. In other words, that marginal gear placement will still be marginal, even if we have spent hours visualising it holding to give us confidence!

The factors below are all important when preparing for fall practice, but they will also stand you in good stead when thinking about leading. Getting into the habit of working systematically through each risk factor is good practice in facing up to risk, in itself beneficial as it is avoidance that tends to maintain anxiety.

UNDERSTAND THE MECHANICS OF GEAR, BOLTS AND ROPE

If you have any question marks in your mind about the gear side of things, I strongly advise you to seek advice or training from a qualified mountaineering and climbing instructor (MCI; or international equivalent) who can talk you through the mechanics of how everything works, and check your gear placements and rope management. Whilst this might seem like an unnecessary expense if you have been climbing a while, if you have a question mark in your mind when leading or falling about whether everything will hold, then your investment will pay dividends in knowing that actually, everything will work as it should.

SITUATIONS FOR PRACTISING FALLS

Many climbers start by practising falls at the climbing wall or gym, but as you progress you may move to being at outdoor venues. Consider the physical risk elements – where are you going to fall, what obstacles are in the flight path, where will you land, how will you get back on the wall afterwards? Importantly for outdoor practice, how will you minimise wear and tear on bolts and gear? Think about your worries in relation to each of these factors – how much do you worry about it, and how likely is it to happen? How can you minimise the risks associated with each factor, or find out if your fears are likely or unlikely?

PSYCHOLOGICAL AND SOCIAL RISKS

This is very personal to you, but some climbers worry about shouting, swearing or crying during fall practice, so you will need to factor this into your risk assessment as by not doing so, there is extra pressure and stress which might inhibit your session. Being prepared for the psychosocial risks might mean being open and honest with your climbing partner, and finding ways to manage any embarrassment from involuntary noises rather than avoiding the wall for the next month.

SAFETY AND BUDDY CHECKS

Finally, having a system of buddy checks is important. Checking each other's knots, rope, harness and belay device, as well as communicating clearly about the practice and what is going to happen when, will ensure a smoother practice. It can also form a kind of pre-climb routine, giving a rhythmic and predictable start to the climb which can help settle the nerves. Always have a final check that the fall height and landing zone are safe and there is no one on a route which crosses onto yours right underneath you before embarking on your practice (yes this can happen!).

LANDING PRACTICE

Being comfortable with landing is really important from a physical safety point of view and also to make a relaxed landing position automatic. If you haven't taken many falls, then you won't have had much opportunity to practise landing. Try hanging on a rope and bouncing around on the wall. Get comfortable with landing with a bend in your knees and try not to grip the rope with your hands; extra hand or shoulder tension will signify extra stress to the brain. Keep your head up and your eyes open for obstacles, and try to stay loose with steady breathing. You can extend this practice by breathing out as you land, keeping your body soft and loose, and try a cue word such as 'land' or 'bounce' that you can begin to associate with the practice. Practise in the same way whenever you can, on autobelays, when being lowered off, etc.

Remember, try not to grip the rope (you don't need to hold onto the rope; the rope is holding onto you remember!), breathe out, and keep your legs soft and supple. Practise bouncing from side to side and in more difficult places (e.g. corners, traverses) so you get some variety in your practice. You can also practise landing when bouldering, again taking the strain by bending your knees, breathing out as you land, and allowing your body to absorb the shock of the jump or fall. As you progress, you'll be able to switch from bouncing around or jumping off, to practising landing from unexpected falls in situations where you feel safe, before tackling lead or more scary falls. This is covered in the next chapters.

SUMMARY

You've worked on some of the key elements of feeling safe to fall, apart from falling itself. You should now have a good sense of trust in your belayer, the gear and rope systems, and practised landing well. You have identified what makes a good objective risk assessment, as well as some of the more personal psychological factors which contribute to your own perception of risk. You may also have had some important conversations with your climbing partner about co-creating a true climbing partnership, taking charge of your own climbing needs. We are now ready to move forward to tackle the big challenge – working on the fear of falling.

CHAPTER **7**

Undertaking fall practice indoors

If you've skipped ahead to this chapter without reading the preceding ones, go back now and read them. The reasons for this are: (a) falling practice is not suitable for everyone and you should not undertake it without consulting a professional if you have a history of trauma, accidents or bad belaying experiences; (b) you first need in place good anxiety management skills (see chapter 5) since you must practise falling in a relaxed state, or it will do more harm than good; (c) you need to be aware of all the ways climbers and coaches often get falling practice wrong, or you will do more harm than good (see the end of this chapter) and (d) you need to be able to trust your belayer, the system and accurately appraise the risks of undertaking any fall practice before starting out (chapter 6).

BEFORE YOU START

Before you start on any falling practice, make sure that

1. You understand the risks involved and can accurately assess your fall zone and the safety of all the equipment you are using.
2. That your belayer is able to give you a soft, safe catch and understands the best way to keep you safe as you fall.

3. You have learnt the anxiety management techniques well and practised them enough both off and on the wall/rock.
4. You do not have any accidents, trauma or bad belaying incidents in your history (if so, please seek advice from a sport or clinical psychologist before undertaking falling practice).
5. You have performed all the safety checks, buddy checks, and have had a clear conversation with your belayer, so you both know the plan for the falling practice.

THE PRINCIPLES OF EXPOSURE WORK FOR FEAR OF FALLING

With those caveats in place, it is important to understand the principles of how exposure or systematic desensitisation works in order to get falling practice right. The aim with any exposure work is to pair relaxation with a feared stimulus or situation. I'll say that again – you need to learn how to *relax* whilst falling, otherwise you will simply be rehearsing and amplifying a fear of falling.

Exposure work comes from behavioural models which link back to the principles of classical conditioning and operant conditioning – think Pavlov and his dogs, who began to salivate whenever they heard a bell ring, simply because they learnt to associate the bell with the arrival of food. Pavlov paired a previously neutral and unrelated cue (the bell ringing) with an involuntary conditioned response (salivating). Operant conditioning involves pairing a voluntary behaviour with a response/consequence (Skinner taught rats to press a lever (cue) in order to get food (response/consequence). Classical and operant conditioning models have been used extensively in helping people overcome fears and phobias, and have a good evidence base.[1] The main way exposure therapies are thought to work are by helping people to pair the cues for their fear or phobia (in our case falling), with a different and competing response (relaxation – you cannot be relaxed and scared at the same time, hence 'competing'), so they can begin to habituate (get used to) to a previously feared situation.

The procedure is to teach climbers relaxation skills first, then develop a hierarchy of their fears, and starting with the least feared situation, to gradually expose them to it whilst practising a relaxed body response – hence the name. It is thought to work in two ways; first you start to undo the avoidance associated with the feared situation and the climber learns to cope with it; and second, it is thought to alter the neural pathway associated with the feared situation, where instead it is associated with bodily signs of relaxation rather than tension, fear and anxiety. In systematic desensitisation and exposure, there may also be an imagined component, whereby you start off by simply imagining the feared situation and pairing it with relaxation, and gradually move into real-life practice.

Whilst some climbers and coaches advocate taking a few really big whippers to get to grips with a fear of falling, there is no research evidence (but some anecdotal evidence) that this is a helpful approach, and it's only palatable for some people. The reason for this is it is more akin to a technique called flooding, something that was used for some phobias but has largely been found to be less effective than exposure work or systematic desensitisation. In flooding, the person needs to stay in the *most* feared situation for as long as possible, until they become accustomed to it and their fear subsides. Research evidence found that flooding as a technique was often too difficult for clients to undertake and if effective, the results did not tend to last as long.[2] It is possible that rather than becoming accustomed to the feared situation, the clients entered a state of learned helplessness[3] and gave up trying to escape it physically, instead trying to switch off mentally. This is not the same as becoming used to something in a good way, rather the opposite.

It is quite difficult to replicate flooding properly in climbing, partly because the nature of falling is that it can only go on for so long till the rope catches, so you are not in a freefall state for long enough to get used to it before it ends. It is also only a palatable option to a few climbers, and most will find it so aversive that they will not continue taking large falls for long enough to get used to it. So in short, my recommendation is that you do not opt for flooding as a method of overcoming a fear of falling, but instead go for the longer-term, step-by-step approach of graded exposure to your fears hierarchy.

DEVELOPING A FEARS HIERARCHY

Having already established a good anxiety management skill set, it's time to brainstorm every single situation where you worry about falling (or not being caught!) and every type of fall that bothers you. I find the easiest way to do this is to use Post-its or summary cards or similar, and put one feared situation onto each card, since next you are going to order them from least scary to most scary. Be sure to include things like watching other climbers fall if this bothers you, to dropping into your harness at the top of a route without first waiting for the rope to come tight on you, the point just before you fall, or going for hard insecure moves on a top rope. If you've ever hesitated about going for it, you need to list the characteristics of that scenario for your hierarchy. There is an example below to help stimulate your thinking;

Example falling fears hierarchy

Increasing scariness ↑

Trad lead fall

Traverse fall when seconding trad

Above the bolt lead fall

Threading the rope on a sport climb and lowering into my harness when belayed by someone I don't know well

Below the bolt sport climb fall

Falling off a high boulder

Lowering to sit in my harness on a trad belay

Taking a fall on a trad top rope

Taking a fall on a top rope at the gym

Watching other climbers take a lead fall

Tentative/delicate moves on a slab on a loose top rope

Watching the film 'On Sight'

What's interesting about this exercise is how often taking a fall from above a bolt on the lead is way up on the hierarchy, and how a whole host of other more subtle worries are often below it, so starting with lead climbing falls often misses out many other important feared situations. Many climbers also have habits which have become ingrained which work against them when it comes to leading. For example, if you can only hang in your harness when you are certain that the rope has been pulled tight in, you are effectively teaching yourself to only feel safe with a tight rope. Similarly, many climbers will agree that they feel safest when top roping, and yet still feel reluctant to truly commit to insecure moves where they are uncertain of the outcome. Instead they may say 'take' before trying, or make a half-hearted effort, kidding themselves that they have really gone for it. In essence here, it is the lack of control that is feared, instead of or in addition perhaps to the fall. It can be helpful to have your belayer observe you when climbing, looking for hesitations (perhaps on sideways moves), calls of 'watch me' and other tell-tale signs such as looking down to check the knot or belayer.

Exercise: Losing the pull on the harness

One of the key things climbers often don't realise is that they have got used to climbing and dropping with a pull on their harness from a snug rope. This means that a key kinaesthetic cue for safety (the pull) is missing when they are lead climbing, and that makes anxiety levels shoot up before they even leave the floor. This exercise is all about learning how to feel safe without that pull on the harness.

1. *Start by climbing on a slightly looser top rope than you would normally have on some easy climbs, and then gradually increase the difficulty of the climb. If you feel any twinges of anxiety (scores of 4+ on the anxiety scale), then pause, use your breathing and muscle release, or a grounding technique to help lower your anxiety levels. Do not climb on until your anxiety levels are less than 4/10.*
2. *Repeat this exercise with progressively harder climbs. Notice when you want to ask for a tighter rope and try to sit on this urge. Make*

sure your belayer knows in advance that this is what you want to do so they don't inadvertently scupper you! Autobelays are also great for this kind of practise as you never get a pull on the rope.

3. *At the top of any climb, you have the opportunity to simply drop onto the rope and have your belayer catch you. Providing your belayer knows this is what you are going to do, then you can work together to eliminate that waiting to be pulled in tight before lowering off. Try not to look down to check what they are doing, simply breathe out, relax your muscles and slump onto the rope. Ask your belayer to keep you up there until you feel relaxed enough to be lowered (again scores of less than 4/10). Keep breathing from your belly, tensing and releasing any tight muscles, and try not to grab the rope.*

The aim here is to feel safe without the sensation of a pull on your harness from the rope. If you have had a lot of scary leading experiences, then you will want to lead climb at the lowest level you feel comfortable with for quite some time, until you have plenty of good experiences in the memory bank of feeling safe whilst leading with no harness pull. Think of a ratio of 10 positives to every 1 negative experience for a clue as to how much practice you will need at this.

SUDS

For each step on the hierarchy, you need to rate how scary you find it using a scale of 0–10, where 10 is terrifying and 0 is totally relaxed. This is called the Subjective Unit of Distress, or SUDS, and we use this to measure whether the exposure is working, how long to keep going for and how to know when to move on to the next stage of the process. What normally happens during exposure work is your anxiety gets worse before it gets better, in that you may find that your SUDS scores go up slightly as you begin the work, but after some time, they should start to come back down again within that session. Ideally, you want to keep going in that session until your SUDS score is around 3 out of 10 or less. You may need several sessions to achieve this, and so it is really important not to rush and to really focus on consolidation of each step.

BEFORE YOU START EACH EXPOSURE SESSION

After picking the step of the hierarchy to work on, risk assessing and measuring your SUDS, the next thing to do is to start with a short relaxation practice. You can use whatever skill you found most helpful from chapter 4, but be sure to fully focus on it, rather than half-heartedly going through the motions whilst thinking about what you are about to do next. I find the easiest exercises to do before starting up the wall are some long slow breaths out, a shortened version of the progressive muscle relaxation – shoulder shrug for example – and the soles of the feet, where you ground yourself into your feet. Then redo these before you get to the point of the planned fall/jump.

TAKING THE PLUNGE(!)

Try to breathe out as you fall/jump, and drop your shoulders. Avoid gripping the rope if you can since this puts more tension through the hands and shoulders and it's also a psychological safety behaviour (see chapter 4) – you couldn't hold yourself onto the rope even if your knot undid, so it's non-essential. Keep your eyes 'soft' and aware of hazards around you. Your legs and knees should be bent slightly in front you, with the aim to absorb the impact. It can help to have a cue word such as 'absorb' or 'bounce' to help you. As you land, focus on steadying your breathing through again breathing out slowly. And repeat, for as long as you are able to, and until you feel your SUDS level decreasing. By the end of the session, your SUDS level should be lower than when you started.

KNOWING WHEN TO END THE PRACTICE SESSION

Try to be clear in your own mind whether you are ending the practice because you truly feel your SUDS have decreased to a minimal score of 3 or less out of 10, or whether you have simply had enough. The latter is avoidance and will mean that you probably should keep going longer; however, if your SUDS level has been increasing throughout, this is probably a sign that something has gone awry in your practice, and you likely need to step back down a few levels. Regardless of the reason why you are stopping, it is important to stay up high until your breathing is back to normal, your heart rate is down and you feel relaxed. This may mean hanging in your harness for quite some time – 20 minutes is not uncommon – until you have low SUDS scores. The reason for this additional step at the end of the practice is so you only leave height when relaxed. This is to avoid going into 'flight' or escape mode when high up on the wall. Leaving the situation in a state of high physiological alert (pounding heart, fast breathing and tense muscles) creates a conditioning effect where being up high is associated with anxiety, and can create a further problem whereby all climbing becomes associated with scary falling practice effects, 'leaking' the anxiety into the climbing more generally.

MOVING ON TO THE NEXT STEP

It's hard to predict when any climber will be ready to try the next step on their fears hierarchy, but it is wise to err on the side of over-consolidation, rather than being impatient and rushing ahead too quickly. As a rule of thumb, you need to feel almost bored before moving ahead. For some people this might take three practice sessions, for some it may take weeks, and it may differ at different steps of the hierarchy in line with the level of fear experienced. So the first steps may be overcome more quickly than those later on. It can also be hard to know whether you are inadvertently avoiding some of the mental elements of the situation, perhaps by avoiding thinking about the drop, or deliberately not looking down as you fall as that heightens your sense of fear. It's easy to kid ourselves we have done all we need to do when it's a scary situation!

Even if you feel you are ready to move on, it's worth spending the first part of a practice session consolidating the previous session, so stepping back down the hierarchy and practising at a lower level than your last session is a good way to start. Expect to have a kind of bumpy decrease in your anxiety between sessions; that means, you will have some slight increases in your anxiety at the beginning of a new session, but by the end of the session, your anxiety should be lower than when you started. Overall, the trend should be that your SUDS are decreasing; if they are not, then stop, and re-evaluate your practice.

Climber Study: Thelma

Thelma had spent some time learning the anxiety management principles and then applying them in clip-drop practices and working up to small falls from above the bolt. She felt pretty comfortable doing this, but she was still feeling fearful on the lead and tended to shout 'take' or downclimb and take a jump onto the bolt. During the consultation, we figured out that the importance of being in control was one of her core beliefs, and observation of her top roping something a few grades harder than her redpoint grade revealed that she was not able to take a natural fall. So, although Thelma had got really good at jumping off, she had not yet got comfortable with unexpected falls. We worked out a hierarchy for uncontrolled or natural falls, and she started with getting on hard routes on top rope, then on the autobelay, before slowly progressing natural falls below the bolt and so on. She also worked off the rock on some of the thoughts around being out of control, trying to figure out what was so bad about it for her and whether her fears were justified or helpful, and ways to unhook from those thoughts when they happened.

PROBLEMS WITH FALLING PRACTICE

It's worth noting that sometimes, what looks like a fear of the sensation of falling, is actually a combination of other fears. Fear of being out of control; fear of the unknown; fear of being seen to make a mistake; fear of making a fool of ourselves; lack of trust in the belayer; gear or bolts; and, for many people, fear of fear itself. This is why I find it so frustrating that the common solution proposed to this multitude of fears is simply to fall off more – and what's often actually practised is jumping off (rather than actually falling). In this section I will explore some of the problems with falling practice and what your practice should actually look like. A healthy fear of falling can be helpful, and it may persist despite our sense of it being 'irrational' due to how safe modern gear is. It is worth pointing out again that falling practice is not the only way to overcome a fear of falling.

I think we have to speculate a little as to why falling practice is so popular, given there is no research evidence out there to support it. Perhaps within our climbing culture and mainstream culture, there persists the idea that climbers are brave, courageous or even crazy, descriptions which don't match anxious, scared or cautious. Perhaps we climbers enjoy the experience of confronting and overcoming or controlling our fears and emotions,[4] and feeling fearful doesn't necessarily chime with that drive. Also, falling practice is quite literally in every book on climbing or coaching climbing. People don't seem to be speaking up about how falling practice has not helped them or has actively made them worse, so it appears to be some kind of shameful secret when climbers cannot seemingly overcome their fears.

I've already mentioned that a fear of falling and heights are kind of hard-wired into us, and so we are trying to overcome centuries of evolution in habituating to falling. The common question climbers have is, why does this fear of falling kick in during what they would term 'safe' routes where the objective risk is low? But focusing only on objective risk (of injury or death) ignores the innate and aversive nature of the sensation of falling, and also all the subjective risks. Subjective risks can include fear of losing control, of social embarrassment and so on. As social animals, often it is our own response to feeling afraid and that being witnessed by others which causes us some anxiety and embarrassment.

So our whole concept of a fear of falling being irrational is unhelpful, because without acceptance of this fear, we will not find good solutions and coping strategies to overcome it. Many climbers do not and never will find the sensation of falling anything other than unpleasant or anxiety-provoking, particularly when they fall a long way. So falling practice may never do what it intends to do, if falling is loaded with evolutionary aversive sensations. However, there can also be problems in the way that falling practice is carried out, which can also hamper the habitation process.

FALLING IS NOT PAIRED WITH RELAXATION

This crucial step of learning relaxation skills first and ensuring that any falling practice is carried out in a relaxed way is often missed out. So falling practice is undertaken with feelings of stress, anxiety and even fear. What this does then is exacerbate feelings of fear around falling, and for some people this then translates into a fear of leading even very easy routes, or even climbing itself. Any falling practice must be carried out with relaxed breathing, relaxed muscles and relaxed thought processes for it to be effective.

Exercise: Imagined exposure

Many people tense up massively whenever anyone near them or being belayed by them takes a fall, or whenever they think about taking a fall themselves. This means they are missing multiple opportunities to work on their fear of unexpected falls!

Use the same skills we learnt in the section on how to manage the physical symptoms of anxiety – breathing from the belly, muscle release, grounding techniques. Spend a few minutes using the belly breathing and muscle release to settle yourself.

Note your anxiety score on the thermometer or 0–10

Conjure up the image of the fall in your mind, in as rich detail as possible. It can help to write the situation down here first so you can be sure to include what happened at the end. Commonly people stop their imagined exposure at the point of the fall, never spooling forward to the point where the person lands and is ok.

As you think about the falling situation, keep your breathing steady (focus on the out breath) and your muscles relaxed (tense and release). You can also use a grounding technique such as pushing your feet into the floor to remind yourself this is just a thought and is not happening now. Note your anxiety score at the 'worst' point.

Use some coping statements, e.g. 'it's just words and pictures in my mind', 'I'm ok where I am' and 'and they were fine at the end'. Be sure to play the film in your mind until the end where the person starts to climb again or lowers off. Note your anxiety score at the end. Repeat a number of times for up to 30 minutes, noting your anxiety scores every time.

At the end of your exposure session, do a slightly longer breathing and muscle release session. Note down anything you found tricky, and also be sure to write down how well you did by tackling this fear.

FALLING IS NOT PRACTISED FOR LONG ENOUGH OR OFTEN ENOUGH

Another issue with the way falling practice is typically conducted is it is often done for too little time and without enough consolidation. If a climber finds falling aversive, they will rush from falling below a bolt to falling from above the bolt in a single session, with very few practice attempts. Some climbers advocate just taking a huge fall to 'get it over and done with', but this is very often so scary that they quit straight after and lower off in a state of high anxiety. Climbers may also undertake falling practice just a few times a year, which is unlikely to be often enough to truly learn how to relax when falling. In true exposure work, exposure to the feared situation should continue until the anxiety subsides; this is difficult to achieve with falling where the actual scary part (just before and during the fall) might last seconds, and needs to be repeated over and over for the anxiety to dissipate. Most climbers and belayers struggle to keep going long enough for this to really occur.

IT'S JUMPING, NOT FALLING

Most climbers practise falling by jumping off rather than by actually falling off. Falling off and jumping off are usually exercising two slightly different skills and fear buttons. In jumping off practice, the climber is in control of when and how to fall. Jumping off practice can be effective if the issue is just needing to get used to the sensation of falling itself, or as a rung on the ladder of exposure. However, if a climber (also) fears being out of control, then jumping off practice will not give exposure to that feared scenario; they will need to climb something too hard for them in order to take a natural fall without being in control of when it happens. It can be really hard even then to allow a fall to occur naturally, with many climbers kidding themselves that they have tried as hard as they can to stay on the route, when in fact they have given up and allowed themselves to let go, in order to maintain at least a tiny bit of control.

Exercise: Overcoming the need to stay in control

1. *Get on some top rope climbs which are 'too hard' for you. Practise trying super hard on these routes to the point of taking a natural fall. Watch out for making half-hearted attempts but protectively and pre-emptively choosing to let go rather than slipping off the hand or footholds. Also watch out for saying 'take' before you have tried the move. This needs to be a regular part of your practice, and who knows, you may surprise yourself by climbing harder than you expected!*

2. *Practise climbing as fast as you can up some routes within your capability. Speed walls are ideal for this as you can time yourself and try to beat your time, but any autobelay or superslick belayer will do! You are aiming to go as fast as you possibly can, over-riding your thoughts and just letting your body climb. Again, you may surprise yourself by climbing better than you expected!*

3. *If you like to be in control, typically that goes with worries about making mistakes and messing up sequences. On a top rope, practise climbing 'first touch' – that is simply holding the handhold in the first way you grasp it without readjusting, or placing the foot and keeping it wherever it lands until you move off it. The aim here is not to over control the sequence.*

4. *Climbing games can also be a fun way to tackle the need to stay in control. In the bouldering wall, have your partner tap the holds you need to take. Or, have a game of 'add a move', where each person adds a new move into the sequence. Other games where you limit the use of one hand, a foot or are blindfolded can be fun ways to loosen up a little, provided you feel safe to do so. It is, however, important that these experiences do not add to the bank of negatives in your mind, so make sure that the difficulty level of the climbs is easy and/ or that you feel confident and safe doing them.*

NO EXPOSURE TO THE POINT BEFORE THE FALL

For most climbers, the point *just before they fall* is the most scary part and the anticipation is often worse than the fall itself. However, this is rarely factored into falling practice, and so again climbers may not be exposing themselves to the real fear trigger. In practice, it can be difficult to elongate the moment before a fall in a gradual way, but it is possible to simply try to hang on for as long as possible before naturally falling off. What is tricky with this practice is to stay relaxed as you hang on! Muscles will naturally tighten, breathing will tend to quicken or breath holding will occur. As far as possible even when hanging on in this practice, it is important to breathe from the belly and to relax any muscles not required for hanging on. It is also possible to use some mindfulness techniques to observe the thoughts and manage any fearful self-talk, but this is quite an advanced technique and will require some practice and gradual build-up.

LOWERING OFF FEELING VERY STRESSED

In graded exposure, the exposure finishes with the client in as relaxed state as possible, before leaving the stressful situation. In falling practice, most climbers simply lower off as soon as they have taken their last fall, exiting the situation (being up high) with accelerated heart and breathing rates, tight muscles and a sense of relief – all the hallmarks of anxiety – rather a sense of relaxation and confidence from having overcome a step on the fear ladder. What they are doing therefore is actually reinforcing the fact that being up high is scary and being on the ground is safe. Climbers must stay up high, hanging in their harnesses if necessary, until they feel relaxed, in order to exit the situation in a relaxed state.

IT DOESN'T WORK FOR EVERYONE

Whilst falling practice can be helpful for some climbers, it is important to be aware that it's not the only way to reduce anxiety about leading, and indeed for some people, the experience of falling practice can be so aversive that the more they do it, the more they condition themselves to feel anxious about falling rather than overcoming it. Climbers who have had traumatic falls or witnessed or been involved in falling accidents should not use falling practice as the first port of call to overcoming residual fears from the trauma, without first checking that they do not in fact have symptoms of PTSD, since it could make things a lot worse. This is discussed further in the final chapter of this book. There are lots of other ideas throughout this book for other mental techniques to work on that will improve your confidence and climbing, even if falling practice is not right for you.

Climber Study: Jay

Jay went on a sport climbing holiday and was encouraged by friends to try falling practice to overcome their fear of falling. They took progressively bigger falls, but found that their anxiety continued to increase through the week, so that by the end of the week, they were barely able to lead at all. Everyone was mystified as to why this was the case.

On assessment, we discovered that Jay really hated the sensation of falling, and found it hard to trust the belayer, even though they were competent. As the week wore on, they then started to fear the bolt placements might rip out, the rope might snap and so on, with some fairly serious mental images to go with it. Their fear became broader the more they fell off. Jay was tending to hold their breath, grip the rope and keep looking down at the belayer, all of which were contributing to a negative experience.

We started by going through some anxiety management techniques in some detail, and using these when climbing, keeping the climbing super easy. If at any point Jay got scared, they paused, used the anxiety management techniques and waited until their anxiety decreased substantially before deciding whether to continue or come down. This rehab took some time, but Jay was able to start leading again, and later used some different techniques to keep focused on the climbing rather than worrying about falling, since further falling practice was not appropriate for them.

SUMMARY

This chapter has focused more on sport climbing/gym climbing for optimum fall practice, as this is the simplest environment to control and the one where most climbers begin to work on their fear of falling. Keys points to remember are: always learn the anxiety management techniques first as you must pair any falling/jumping practice with relaxation, or you will simply be reinforcing any falling anxiety. Second, build a clear hierarchy of feared falls, and take your time working through each level, making sure to consolidate – you must be patient and play the long game here for lasting results. Finally, be aware that there can be a broad gulf between expected 'falls'/jumping practice and taking real, natural and unexpected falls, and practising the first does not necessarily impact on the second much.

Whilst falling practice is often carried out with good intentions, it is vital that climbers understand the reasons for their fear, as well as how to carry out graded exposure correctly, so they do not inadvertently make their fears worse. Falling practice as it is typically conducted has a number of inherent problems, and is not the solution for some climbers, who might be best advised to try other techniques for helping them to focus on the climbing rather than the falling. The next chapter will cover adapting falling practices for bouldering and trad climbing, and exercises to move your sport climbing practices on further when outdoors.

CHAPTER 8

Adapting falling practice for outdoor sport climbing, bouldering or trad

Whilst it would be nice to think that fall practice indoors transfers easily into improved calmness outdoors, that's not necessarily the case! The environment, risks and differences between how we climb indoors and outdoors can really impact on the generalisability of the skills learnt inside. This chapter is designed to give you some ideas about how to continue a successful indoor practice into the outdoors.

FIRST THINGS FIRST – SAFETY

Given the increase in risk factors outdoors compared to indoors (rock quality, weather, appropriateness of the gear for the environment, increased distractions and so on), as ever, if you have any doubts about your ability to assess the risks inherent in these factors, please seek advice from a qualified mountaineering and climbing instructor (MCI; or international equivalent). This is not simply sensible from an objective risk point of view, but also figuring out the risks and your own ability to deal with them will give you confidence from a psychological point of view. Whilst it's natural to want to avoid thinking about risks, we are left with a nagging sense of doubt at the back of our minds, and this avoidance then does not allow for risk mitigation or contingency planning. Spending half an hour walking around a new crag; noting any loose rock, descents, type of gear best suited to the rock and checking you have it with you; observing for any crazy practices by other climbers (!) and figuring out your own exit points from your route is time well spent as it will allow you mentally put these worries to bed. If you don't like what you see in one of these areas, talk to your climbing partner about it. Is there anything you can do to mitigate the risk? What are both of your views on the potential likelihood and possible impact of this risk? Do you need to alter your plans? It is also important to do this at familiar and well-known venues in case there has been a change in the rock stability, though in my experience it is harder to notice small changes in risk at familiar venues since we tend to have a lower level of vigilance when we feel we 'know' the place well.[1]

GOOD PRACTICE/ETHICS

The second factor to bear in mind is how to minimise your impact on the venue, rock and other climbers if you are undertaking any 'unusual' practices here. For example, if you are going to be taking repeated practice falls on a sport route, consider the potential wear on the bolts; spread the falls across a number of different bolts, if top roping be sure to use your own karabiner/maillon at the top, and if you are practising sitting on gear, can you find an out-of-the-way crack on an unmarked bluff instead of a route? For bouldering, always consider the environmental impact of chalk/chalk spillage, and mat placements. And be aware that if there are other climbers nearby, that you may well be destroying their concentration! However, that should not put you off doing the practices you need; you do have as much right to be there as anyone else. Usually, waiting till they have finished their route, or having a quick hello and explaining what you are going to be doing and why, is enough to ease everyone's day.

OUTDOOR SPORT CLIMBING

Outdoor sport climbing probably has the closest resemblance to indoor wall lead climbing, and so many of the practices will be the same. Clearly you will need to consider wear and tear on bolts and anchors and the impact on other users of the crag, but perhaps the main issue will be getting the rope up to a safe height for taking falls when there are limited easy route options.

This is where a clip stick comes into its own. You can also use stiffened slings adapted to become quick draws to extend your reach, either bought (such as the Edelrid Aramid slings) or I've seen people use home-made ones, using a baton taped to their quick draw, then swapped with a regular draw once you've made the bolt. Another option includes lowering off a neighbouring route and swinging across to put the quick draws in and clip another rope trailed from you whilst you climbed up, clipped in at a suitable height. Again the advice above regarding wear and tear holds true, and make sure you use the principles of physical relaxation as you lower onto the bolt, or jump or fall, so that you can pair relaxation with the falling and landing practice.

TRAD CLIMBING

Most of the trad climbers I have worked with, despite focusing on trad for many years, rarely weight their gear except for at belays, and then only partially or reluctantly! If you ask them about how good their gear is, they will usually say it's pretty good, but even so, they have rarely tested it out in any sort of way. There is something rather wonderful about seeing the change in their face as they tentatively lower onto a single nut, holding their breath, changing to relief as the nut holds and they realise that these metal bits and bobs actually do work! If this is you, then there is a lot of confidence to be gained from some systematic 'sitting' practice.

Exercise: Sitting on your gear on a simulated lead

This exercise is easiest with three people, with the leader here doing a simulated lead. On an out-of-the-way bluff, find a crack that allows you to place lots of pieces of gear and has a good belay at the top. Have a top rope as your backup line onto the leader and belayed by one person with a slight bit of slack, and then the other belayer belays the lead climber as they climb and clip into the gear.

Now comes the interesting bit! After relaxing your breathing and muscles, sit onto each piece of gear, knowing you have the safety of the backup top rope. The idea here is to be able to sit onto the gear with the lead rope, but with the backup top rope a little slack – it is there in case your gear fails for any reason and to give you confidence to try out the exercise at the start. Remember to breathe out as you sit, and try not to grip the rope or gear. As you gain confidence in your gear, you can choose smaller wires, and to sit with a little more 'bounce'. The key thing here is to stay as relaxed in your body as possible.

If you have had your gear placements checked by an MCI or similar experienced person and have tried out some sitting practice, then you may want to try to some larger falls on gear. I would always advocate that this is done with a safety top rope line, until you are confident that your gear placements work well from various heights, not only from a physical risk point of view, but also to allow you to adjust to falling onto gear psychologically. The principles are the same as outlined in the previous chapters on falling practice indoors; you must be relaxed as you undertake the practice, you must keep going until your SUDS levels drop to a low level, and you must not lower off or top out until you feel relaxed in your body again. In these ways you will ensure that you are not sensitising yourself to falling onto gear. In practice it will be difficult to take natural falls onto gear, unless you pre-place your gear off the top rope first, since getting up a route that is too hard enough to encourage a fall would usually be too risky in terms of placing gear on the lead.

BOULDERING

Fear of falling can be an issue for boulderers too, although in some respects it is simpler in that there are fewer additional elements to deal with, such as trust in belayers and systems. Again, the same principles tend to apply; boulderers are often more comfortable taking planned falls rather than natural falls, and topping out can also be an issue, even easy top outs, if the boulder is a high one. I recall being in Font and getting warmed up on a very straightforward highball problem, and suddenly spooking myself whilst looking down to find a foothold just below the top. Below and to one side the ground dropped away making it seem even higher, and at the bottom was a spiky looking rock. Even though I knew I wouldn't fall in that direction, I could not take my eyes off it and images of myself toppling off sideways and smashing into the spike below were racing through my mind! Eventually, with some 'encouragement' from my friend, I found a hidden handhold on the top and hefted myself on, seal-like, much to my relief, and started to laugh hysterically as I realised I had just fluffed an incredibly easy move because I had my eye on the danger and not on the climbing!

It is worth following the same principles as outlined previously if you find you get worried when bouldering about falling off. Learn the anxiety management skills, create a fears hierarchy and then start to systematically practise the feared situations, whilst trying to stay relaxed. Investing in some good mats/bouldering pads is well worth it, particularly if you boulder on your own a lot; there is no glory in not topping a problem that you know you can do because you didn't have a mat in the right place at the right time! The goal with mat placement is to minimise the physical risks so that you can climb to your max, so having a good walk round and inspecting the problem, where it goes and likely fall points, remembering that as it steepens you will fall further out from the base, is crucial. So again, watch for the trap of avoiding thinking about the risks if they scare you, and instead try to do an objective risk assessment, and then take good mitigating steps so you can free your mind up to focus on the climbing.

Getting used to jumping off onto the mat from various heights and angles will be a start here, again remembering to breathe out and land with bent knees, and allow your body to absorb the fall. If you are very nervous, you are likely to hold tension in your body which will make for a stiffer landing. If you are bouldering in company and want a spotter, it's worth talking to them about how you want to be spotted. Their job, of course, is only to help you to land on the mat squarely, but do you want them to talk to you, stay quiet, firmly guide you to the mat or just stand well back and only step in if it looks like you are going to hit your head? Having these conversations is just as important in bouldering as in trad or sport climbing.

For getting used to height, then climbing up and down multiple times, keeping your body relaxed, and progressively going a little higher each time, is a good way to adjust to the height mentally. If at any point you start to feel anxious, then trying to pause for a moment, breathing out and relaxing any muscles not currently in full use, before deciding whether to continue or not, is helpful.

Topping out is often a big issue, so again here the key is to watch out for 'summit fever' where you just want the problem to be over! This tends to be due to fight-or-flight-type behaviour, and you are more likely to make a mistake and fumble the top if you start to tip into fight/flight, as your climbing skills will regress slightly under these conditions.[2] Practise pausing before you top out, releasing your breath and any unneeded muscle tension, and take your time if possible to minimise the chance of a slip. Once you commit to the top, then do make sure you commit rather than being half-hearted.

PUSHING YOUR GRADE: THINKING TACTICALLY

There comes a point when it's time to stop 'practising' and commit to trying to integrate all your skills on the lead where there is a possibility of an unexpected natural fall. This is when being strategic and tactical will play dividends. Think about all the elements which might contribute to your anxiety and try to just fight the fire on one front. So, for example, if you feel ok about small falls, then look for a harder, well-bolted climb for example, rather than one with spaced bolts. If exposure is still a problem for you, then don't choose a crag with a steep scree slope below it or a route on an arête, for your first attempt at pushing your climbing. Similarly, pushing your grade at a familiar venue or with a well-trusted partner is more sensible than going all out somewhere you've never been before with a partner you just met on a climbing forum.

Do spend the time planning, rehearsing and visualising a successful ascent (more on this in the imagery chapter). Think about your get-out points and contingency plans if you do find you have bitten off more than you can chew. If this includes setting up a top rope in case you need a rope from above, then don't be ashamed to do this. Have some gear on your harness that you don't mind leaving behind, take your clipstick or your 'cheat draw', and be prepared to lay siege if necessary. When we are breaking through what can feel like a large mental barrier, we do want to stack the odds in our favour. This extends to the right partner, right day, right crag, right route, right fuelling strategy, thorough physical and mental warm-up – the whole nine yards.

Climber study: Sharla

Sharla was a tenacious climber with bucket loads of stamina and technical ability and a preference for sport climbing. But she was struggling to really go for it on the lead. We picked out a F7a, a couple of grades harder than her comfy lead grade, on a well-bolted sport route, after a long period of developing good anxiety management skills. The aim was to push the boat out a little and maybe encourage a natural fall to occur. Sharla clip-sticked up to the second bolt, and had a cheat draw on her harness as a 'just in case'. We couldn't really practise the route as there was no nearby route to set up a top rope on, and also we didn't want Sharla to rehearse the route to death as she usually did!

Sharla mentally broke the route down into bolt-to-bolt sections, and was conscious to bring her anxiety levels down using a breath out and focus word after each clip. Her SUDS levels stayed pretty low overall, and she didn't end up needing her cheat stick! Having the option, however, to hang in her harness if her SUDS came above a 6/10, and knowing she could reach the next bolt from the one she was on, was a great way to break through the F7 barrier without scaring herself too much. We then planned that she would consolidate at this grade, choosing only well-bolted routes for the next 10 sessions, before gradually increasing the challenge levels again.

SUMMARY

Taking your falling practice outdoors requires more judgement about safety, risk, ethics and the impact on other users than any indoor practice. However, the psychological principles remain the same; the focus should be on getting a detailed hierarchy of fears, learning the anxiety management skills and applying them by carrying out any practice in as relaxed state as possible. If you have any question marks or doubts about your gear placements, rock stability, bolts or anchors, rope management or judging where to place bouldering mats relative to height and boulder angle, then do consult with an appropriately qualified climbing or bouldering coach. It is a false economy to carry on with doubts in mind, not just from a safety point of view, but because these doubts will linger unless you confront them, nagging away in the back of your mind and curtailing your performance.

CHAPTER **9**

The social side of climbing

Your climbing performance doesn't happen in a social vacuum. Despite being an individual rather than a team sport, for roped climbing we are dependent on our climbing partners for our safety, and we are often climbing in front of others at the gym or crag. Our climbing community feels close-knit, which can be lovely and supportive, but can also increase worries about being judged by others around them when climbing.

There are also many social nuances to negotiate when climbing – who chooses which route to try, who goes first/who leads first, how many attempts you get, how long you take, when it's your turn to try that boulder problem and that's before even thinking about trusting your life to your belayer, being watched by others, whether you are 'good enough' to try a classic route or problem of that grade, and the sense of belonging to a small community where everyone knows everyone else! You may even bump into an elite climber at a crag or indoor wall, and so the sense of it being a small world is amplified when your heroes inhabit the same spaces as you.

We are social creatures and it has been an evolutionary advantage to fit into a social group for survival – feelings of embarrassment and shame evolved to make sure we toed the line and stayed in the 'in' group. Social comparison then is normal and natural, as is the sense of worry if for some reason you feel you don't quite fit in – we are designed to want to fit in! However, whilst these niceties can make us a good, supportive crag partner (and a nice person generally), if we pay too much attention to them when we are actually climbing, then our climbing can suffer.

Many women seem to feel this particularly acutely, especially if they are in a relationship with someone who climbs harder than them. The tendency can be to let the harder climber make all the decisions, and to organise the climbing session around their needs and goals. Perhaps climbing's outward persona of being a macho or male sport amplifies hidden gender norms; undoubtedly things are changing, but many women still feel a greater lack of confidence in relation to their climbing than men do (e.g. women generally underestimate their abilities compared to men[1]), and worry more about what others think of them. This means they are less likely to take charge of their own climbing sessions, and to feel they have an equal right to the climbing space.

This worry does apply not only to women but to any climber who feels they don't quite fit in for whatever reason. Older climbers, climbers of colour, trans climbers, larger climbers, climbers who 'only' top rope, gym climb or stick to easy climbing, and those from non-climbing backgrounds can have a harder time feeling like they belong in the climbing world. The stereotypes of a young, lean, white male or female, in skimpy clothing/top off, are perpetuated by media images which consistently show this demographic. Getting into the systemic issues which affect climbing is outside the scope of this book, and indeed climbing is only just waking up to its lack of inclusion of diversity, but it is important to acknowledge that social barriers to climbing exist both in our own minds, and in the imagery, structures, attitudes of the community and opportunities to climb, which are not afforded equally to all. This section is going to deal with internal social barriers to climbing well, but this does not mean that the climbing community does not have work to do from a systemic perspective, and we can all play a part in that challenge.

SOCIAL COMPARISON

To climb well, we need full focus on ourselves, and our own climbing movement. If half our mind is preoccupied with what others are thinking, how long we are taking, with questions about why we can't send this route but Ally can, then the doubts, embarrassment and even shame, will start to interfere with our ability to climb. Often climbers use a strategy of trying not to think about these worries, and to push the thoughts and feelings away. The problem, however as we know, is this strategy rarely works for long, and any short-term relief is quickly overtaken by the rebound effect from those worries coming back stronger than ever. If a climber continues to have very negative experiences in this way, then the response can be to start avoiding busy walls, seeking out only less popular crags or only trying well-practised routes where there is little chance of failure if others are around. Over time, our climbing comfort zone begins to shrink as we stick to only routes we are certain we can send, limiting our choices and our opportunities for growth.

Social comparison can go one step further and turn into jealousy of others and a sense of continuous competition with other climbers. Competitiveness is not necessarily a problem in itself if it spurs you on to try harder, but if the comparisons mean you only feel good when others fail, or you often fall short of your own yardstick and spiral into self-criticism, than this is not great for motivation or self-esteem. Positive competitiveness,[2] where we push ourselves and others to improve for the sake of mastery, has a very different feel to some kind of pecking order, where your position in that hierarchy determines whether you are a 'good' or 'bad' climber or person.

It would not be possible to entirely get rid of social concerns – indeed to do so would likely make us a pretty unpopular climbing or life partner! But, it is possible to challenge the thoughts and comparisons so they become more proportionate, and to learn how to focus on our own climbing rather than worrying about what others think.

COMMON SOCIAL CONCERNS IN CLIMBERS

There are a few common themes I've seen over the years of coaching climbers, in terms of the social side of climbing. Worries about taking too long on a route or even just to get ready, worries about not climbing hard enough, being unhappy with how you look as a climber or even feeling inadequate in terms of technique or knowledge, are shared by many climbers. The results of this can be varied. Some people will only climb in front of a select few and will leave a crag or wall if it is too busy. For others, they find themselves rushing on routes so as not to hold up the leader or anyone behind them. Some people will only choose routes or problems they know they can climb, or make excuses about why they are not leading a certain grade (injury or tiredness for example), or even inflate the grade they say they climb when talking to others. This is perhaps the most risky strategy, as they may feel forced into climbing routes which they are not ready for or out of their league. There is also the risk of being ostracised if you are found out. Worries about body image are covered in another chapter, but if you don't feel you look like a climber 'should' look, this can inhibit performance in many different ways, as well as sometimes leading to unhealthy patterns of training and eating.

The underlying theme here is having an expectation of things being a certain way – climbing a certain grade, looking a certain way, climbing a certain way. A sense of inadequacy because you feel you should be 'better' in some way as a climber. Whilst undoubtedly this can motivate some people to train more and climb harder, for most people it is unhelpful to hold these expectations and ideals. By definition, you are not accepting of the way things actually are, of your own reality, and that will limit your ability to train in a way that suits your needs.

Climber study: Gus

Gus is a steady VS climber, but tends to climb with a couple of people who climb much harder than him. Whenever it is his turn to lead, he makes an excuse about an old injury and says 'no you go for it, I'm happy to second today', and he ends up seconding routes which are at the very top of his current ability and finding them pretty tough. All his experiences outdoors are at the very edge of his comfort zone, and he finds the whole thing stressful as he is trying to hide the fact that this route is a bit too hard for him. He rarely has a fun day at the crag, and rather than finding that seconding harder routes helps him improve, his motivation dips and he doesn't allow himself to take his time to work out the moves and improve his technique. His climbing progress plateaus and soon he finds he dreads going to the crag with his friends. He feels embarrassed and frustrated with himself.

We'll return to some of the difficulties Gus has in a moment, with some exercises that help to park the social worries. For social worries in climbing, we are going to use a combination of CBT techniques and ACT techniques. You'll recall from earlier on that CBT aims to introduce doubt to some of our negative thought patterns, to enhance our commitment to doing things differently and so decreasing our anxiety. ACT, on the other hand, helps us to unhook from some of the negative thoughts and feelings, and focus on moving towards our own values, rather than allowing our worries about what others think to dictate our own behaviour. CBT techniques are helpful off the rock, but ACT techniques are more helpful on the rock, so we will be using both in this chapter.

THOUGHT CHALLENGING

Start by completing the thought record below when you go climbing, noting down any thoughts you have about comparisons with others, worries about being judged and so on. Write them down in your own words, in the way you say them in your own mind. Can you notice any themes or patterns? How sticky or believable is this thought on a scale of 0–100%? How did these thoughts affect your feelings, body symptoms, and what you did as a result (behaviour)?

Thought record

Situation	Mood/ feelings	Negative Thoughts	How believable was the thought? 0–100%	Body symptoms	What did you do as a result? Behaviour?

We often act as though our thoughts were real and true, but it's common to make consistent errors in our thinking based on our previous experiences. It's been helpful for our brains to take shortcuts in thinking, to cut down on the cognitive load and free up capacity for other things, which is fine if the shortcuts are helpful, but not so good if we have developed some unhelpful shortcuts. These unhelpful shortcuts are called cognitive distortions. They might have developed in response to a powerful experience, and then been reinforced over time by the way we behave, where perhaps we never give ourselves the chance to disprove these unwritten rules. As an example, if we fluffed our first outdoor climb, taking a long time and getting really cold in the process, and maybe sensed a bit of impatience from the leader who was freezing at the top, then it's easy to see how we might become paranoid about taking too long on a route. We then make sure we speed through each route as quickly as possible, and never give ourselves the chance to learn that it's fine to take your time with some partners and in summer conditions. Cognitive distortions tend to follow familiar patterns, and there are some examples below.

Exercise: Common thinking errors/cognitive distortions

1. All-or-nothing thinking/polarised thinking

Seeing everything as amazing or terrible – thinking in extremes. For example, either I'm popular, or no-one likes me.

2. Overgeneralisation

Basing all your beliefs on one instance, for example, my coach said I needed to try harder so she thinks I'm lazy.

3. Disqualifying the positive

Also known as 'yes-but'; for example, my friend said I climbed well today but that's just because the problems were easy.

4. Mind reading

Thinking we know what someone else is thinking, for example, Josh didn't talk much today, so he must be really cheesed off with me.

5. Fortune telling

Making predictions based on little evidence, for example, I'll never learn how to dyno, because I'm too short.

6. Catastrophising

Thinking the worst – I dropped a nut today and Sarah will be so cross she'll never want to climb outdoors with me again

8. Emotional reasoning

Thinking your thoughts and emotions are facts. For example, 'I feel rubbish about myself therefore I must be a rubbish climber'.

9. Should statements

Holding too tightly onto expectations, shoulds, musts and oughts; for example, 'A good climber should be able to lead this VS' (and therefore, if you can't then you are not a 'good' climber).

10. Personalisation

Taking the blame, for example, 'I'm too slow and everyone had a rubbish time because of me holding them up'.

There are other thinking errors, but I have selected the ones I see climbers making most commonly. Can you notice which types of thinking errors you tend to make? Can you remember when and where you might have developed this cognitive distortion? How did it help you then? Is it still helping you now?

Going back to our thought record, for each thought, ask, what is the evidence for and against these thoughts? How terrible would it be if it were true? How can you find out if this thought is true or not (a behavioural experiment where you collect data by asking others for example)? What do other people in the same situation think? What does someone you admire think about this situation? What alternative viewpoints might there be?

Your aim here is NOT to persuade yourself that there is nothing to worry about, but rather to cast some doubt on the thoughts to weaken them slightly. If you feel you have been able to cast some doubt on the thoughts, what would a more balanced viewpoint look like?

With Gus's example, he was too embarrassed to say that he was finding the routes hard, and thought that his friends wouldn't want to climb easier routes and therefore would be putting the grade of the route above their desire to climb with him. This was an assumption, an example of the mind reading cognitive distortion. This was relatively easy to fix – all he had to do was tell one of his friends that he was finding their route choices too hard, and could they pick out an easier route next time. Gus had been worried that his friends were only friends with him for his belaying – challenging this thought involved asking, what's the worst that can happen if I ask for an easier route, and do I want to be friends with someone who just wants me as their belayer?

As you can see, completing a thought record, identifying what thinking errors you may be making and challenging some of your negative thoughts are techniques best suited to having pen and paper to hand once you are back at home after climbing. But what do we do about those social worries if they show up when we are actually climbing? That's where ACT comes in.

UNHOOKING FROM THOUGHTS AND FEELINGS

In ACT theory, we tend to be too attached to our thoughts and feelings, and end up fusing with them to the extent that we believe them to be 'true', finding it hard to see our core self as separate from our thoughts and feelings. Indeed, we can come to believe that we *are* our thoughts, rather than our thoughts simply being a product of our brains.

In situations like this, if we have decided that what we love about climbing is a core part of our values and really important to us, and we are therefore committed to climbing, then we can use mindfulness and other tools to unhook and de-fuse from our anxious thoughts and feelings.

If we are worrying about climbing in front of others and the attendant thoughts and feelings, then we might choose to use mindfulness to ground ourselves before we enter the busy climbing wall; we might choose to discuss our (embarrassing) thoughts with our climbing partner to reduce the secrecy and shame associated with them; and we might use some techniques whilst climbing to introduce the observer position on our climbing. These could include saying the thoughts out loud very fast or singing them whilst climbing. If climbing at the wall is difficult due to worries about being judged, we might set ourselves progressively more anxiety-provoking goals of climbing in front of an increasing number of people over the course of a few weeks. This will help us to gain confidence, with the goal of doing what is important, regardless of how we feel inside. After climbing, if we find ourselves ruminating over what others might have thought about us and our climbing performance, then we would use the de-fusion techniques again to unhook from those thoughts (e.g. 'Thanks brain, I'm busy right now getting my dinner') and focus on what is important to us right now (e.g. refuelling after the climb). I've given some examples below of the most common social worries climbers have, and how you might tackle them.

Example 1: Finding it hard to enter a climbing wall or climb in front of other people

First, think about what is the underlying belief. For each negative thought, ask yourself, 'if this were true, what would be so bad about this', or 'what's the worst thing about that?'; for example 'I'm not good enough to climb in front of them' > 'they all climb harder than me' > 'they will think I'm rubbish' > 'they will laugh at me' > 'they won't bother talking to me' > 'they won't like me' > 'no-one likes me' > 'I'll be alone forever'.

Once you feel you have got to the root of the issue, you can ask yourself the following questions;

a. What is evidence for or against this belief?
b. What might others think about this if they knew?
c. What is another way of looking at this?

    d. How likely is this to happen?

    e. How can you test this out?

The aim here is to weaken your underlying belief, rather than convince yourself of the opposite; that is, you are aiming to cast doubt on the belief that you will be alone forever, in this example.

You can also conduct some experiments to gather objective data about your belief and/or undertake graded exposure work. For example, you could try climbing in front of other people who climb different grades, or try climbing easier and harder routes in front of others, and figure out whether they notice or not, whether they talk to you or not, and aim to find out whether the grade you climb makes any difference to others' reactions to you. You can also deliberately make a mess of a problem and see if anyone reacts in any way. Finally, you could even conduct a quick poll on social media or with your friends about whether how hard you climb is linked to how much people like you, for example. The key here is to step back a little and be a detective, viewing your thoughts and beliefs with some scepticism and trying to test out whether they are true or not.

Example 2: Worries about taking too long on a route or problem

Similar to above, you can try to find out what is underneath this worry. Are you worried about holding others up? Do you feel that because you don't climb as hard as others, that their time is more valuable than yours? Is there a hidden belief that the harder you climb, the more 'worthy' you are and the more climbing time you deserve? Are you trying to be less visible for some reason? Sometimes, once we start to unpick our assumptions, we can see them for what they really are, which is just assumptions.

For this worry, you could actually time yourself on a route or getting racked up, or on a problem, and compare it with (a) how long you think you take and (b) how long your climbing partner takes and (c) an average based on three different climbers, for example. Are you really as slow as you think you are?

You can also try deliberately slowing down even more on the routes or problems, and watching to see if anyone's reaction changes, or even just to learn to live with the discomfort of taking your time on a route. If you worry about being slow, sometimes by taking control and slowing it down even more, we can begin to get used to the unpleasant feeling of 'taking too long' or 'being too visible', exposing ourselves to the very thing we wish we weren't, which paradoxically takes the power out of it.

Example 3: Finding it hard to take your turn on a boulder problem

This can stem out of heavily ingrained politeness, or equally worries about whether you belong there or a hidden assumption about who gets to muscle in and who doesn't. If you are at a climbing wall, remember, everyone pays the same entry fee and so has the right to equal use of the centre. It can help some people to make an effort to chat to other people climbing in the same area as you; simple social chit chat, questions about the problem or anything really to break the ice. When asking for people to move out of your way so you can try a problem, or to take your turn if a group are hogging a problem, try not to apologise for your presence! Instead, take a confident posture (head up, shoulders down and back, and make eye contact), and say, 'I'd like a turn on that 6b please' or similar. Avoid being very British 'sorry, err, can I just, err sorry, thank you...' You don't need to be apologetic! You might feel this is more polite, but you are reinforcing in your own mind that you don't really have the right to be there by apologising and not communicating clearly. Your confidence will be enhanced by acting confidently rather than timidly.

Example 4: Worries about what others are thinking about you when actually climbing

The main issue here is that your focus is somewhere behind or out to the side of you, with the sense of everyone's eyes burning into the back of your head, and so your attention is not really on your own climbing. Refocusing techniques are useful here. For example, when you notice your thoughts wandering, bring your focus back to climbing-relevant cues. For example, this means picking up on information that will help your climbing performance. This could be external cues – the look, direction and texture of the holds, scanning ahead in a systematic way, and so on, or internal cues. This might be pushing your feet into the holds and really feeling the hold underneath your toes, paying attention to breathing in a relaxed way, or optimising your body position (for example, bringing your harness into the wall). The aim would be to notice as soon as possible that your mind is wandering to what others are thinking, and to refocus it onto something that will help you actually climb. Our minds do wander, that is normal and natural, but practising bringing your attention and focus back to where you need it to be will pay dividends. For this reason, having a regular mindfulness or meditation practice can be helpful.

Another strategy would be to use the thought-challenging techniques outlined above, and perhaps to conduct a survey at your local crag or in a social media climbing group to find out whether people actually do judge others' climbing. You could ask whether (a) they feel judged and (b) whether they judge others and/or (c) whether they think grade climbed or technique is important in whether to make friends with someone, for example. Whatever is at the root of your worries, ask some questions of others and find out, is this really true? Similarly, you could just take a glance around the wall or crag and at any one time, observe how many people are actually watching the person climbing, and whether they are talking about them or giving any negative reaction. Might it be the case that most people are focused on what they are doing rather than on what other people are doing?

It is really important to actively engage with these techniques rather than trying to shortcut them and thinking to yourself, 'I'm sure no-one is really watching' – by actively testing this idea out, you will have some more objective data, and this can help to undermine your internal doubts. Many climbers are aware in their logical mind that their hidden fears and worries are unlikely to be true, but unless they actively engage in data gathering and working through modifying thoughts, and trying out different ways of behaving in front of others, those fears can persist. My advice – don't shortcut these steps, work through them regularly and systematically, and write down your workings and answers. Having things written down is more powerful than just thinking things through in your mind.

Example 5: Feeling jealous or comparing your own performance to others

As part of our evolutionary make-up, it's natural to compare ourselves with others and weigh our personal 'assets' against other people in our mini tribe. However, just because it's natural (having better assets meant better access to resources and a better chance of survival for caveman and cavewoman!) doesn't mean it is helpful! I've worked with many women who feel this acutely, and it may be more problematic for them than for men, perhaps because being competitive is not something generally encouraged or admired in stereotypical female behaviour, whereas it is generally taken as part of the male psyche to compete. Where this gets interesting is in how legitimate and open you are able to be about your competitiveness. If you feel accepting of it then it is possible to use it as motivation to improve, but if you feel some sense of shame attached to feeling competitive, then that adds a layer of distress and 'ought not' on top.

To turn your compare-and-compete mindset into something more helpful, first, acknowledges its presence. Try out telling people, 'I get a bit competitive sometimes and feel jealous when I can't do things as well as someone else'. Does airing your private worry help to decrease its power? Second, if there is someone you see regularly who activates these jealous feelings, but you don't know them well, try to get to know the person better, as a person, not just as a climber. Often, seeing them as a whole person will enable you to see both their strengths and weaknesses, rather than holding them on a pedestal.

Third, tell them you admire their climbing, and be specific about what it is you admire about how they climb. Ask them to share some tips or tricks as to how they developed that ability to climb off-widths or slopers, or how they stay tenacious when they are scared. Acknowledging their strengths may allow you to learn from them and improve your own climbing. Admit your jealousy if possible to them – we tend to feel jealousy is shameful and therefore to keep it secret. These kinds of secrets grow in power in the dark, and so scary though it is, it is best to open up and talk to someone about these feelings, which will rob them of some of their power.

Fourth, ensure that you are not being selective about their strengths and your own weaknesses; in other words, watch out for thinking errors. Is there something you do as well as or better than they do – in or out of climbing – and are you viewing them as 'all good' and yourself as 'all bad'? Finally, you could try out some of the distancing and defusion techniques discussed earlier. For example, draw this jealous part of yourself as a kind of cartoon character. What do they look and sound like? Can you give them a name? When they show up, remind yourself that it's your jealous story showing up again. Equally you could try singing these thoughts out loud, saying them backwards or in a silly voice, or very fast. Does this have an impact on their power?

Climber study: Greta

Greta had a number of worries about climbing, and was frustrated about not progressing. Her top leading grade was F6b, and she avoided the steep wall at her local climbing gym, where the easiest line was F6b. There was another woman who she didn't know, who she would often see climbing on this section of wall, and Greta would feel jealous and then angry with herself for feeling jealous. After exploring these feelings in a session, we set up some experiments for Greta to try. First she was to go and hang out in the steep wall area, and have a really good look at all the lines, and pick one where she felt she could get to the first clip, without checking the grade. She was then to go climb that first section, once every session for a couple of weeks. We also set the goal that Greta would talk to the other woman and tell her how much she admired her climbing style and technique. As a result of doing this, Greta got to know the other woman and started climbing with her too, which helped reduce her feelings of jealousy. She also felt after a couple of weeks of getting to the first clip on a route in the steep area that she could go a bit higher, and so she began working a route on the steep wall. She started to grow in confidence and realise that she was 'allowed' to climb in the steep area, even though she could 'only' climb F6b.

Example 6: Ruminating afterwards about what you said or did during a climbing session

This is a common fear for people who are relatively new to a group or feel they have landed in a climbing group where they are slightly star struck, perhaps because those people climb harder than they do. There can be a sense of pressure to fit in, to keep up and to hide weaknesses, in order to be accepted as part of the group. Again, this is an old behaviour pattern that would have been useful for our survival when it was imperative to stay within a group due to the dangers in the environment. This evolutionary hangover can make us feel self-conscious and lead us to have an internal postmortem on a day at the crag or a climbing trip, worrying about whether we did or said something silly or embarrassing.

The problem with having a mental replay on loop is that it will seem to amplify anything we are not happy with, and blur out all the things we did well or where we got along just fine. Then we start to over-analyse other people's reactions to us, and become paranoid that perhaps Joe didn't say when you were meeting again because really he didn't want to hang out with you again after you fell off that V2.

The first step here is to recognise that they are just thoughts and may or may not bear any resemblance to reality. Remember that we tend to see the negatives or possible negatives in great detail, and gloss over things that went well, seeing them in a more general way. With these types of thoughts, it is better to try not to get into a mental argument with yourself, since this is unlikely to convince you that you are wrong, but rather to use the defusion techniques to observe your thoughts, and to allow you to see that even though they feel real and powerful, they are in fact just thoughts. A second question to ask yourself is, would I really want to hang out with someone who didn't want to hang out with me because I fell off a V2? Just because someone climbs harder than us doesn't make them a better person or more fun to hang out with, and so it's important to question whether you have the group or another climber on a pedestal, without good reason. Finally, make sure your mental filter is not set on negative – be sure to give your attention in a balanced way to your behaviour and performance, giving what you did well as much attention as those potential slip ups.

Example 7: Feeling judged based on how well you climb

This type of worry maps onto what is commonly described as a fear of failure. However for most people, it is not the failure itself that is the problem, but the fear of what others will think of you if you perform badly. This worry tends to extend outside of just climbing ('they'll think I'm a terrible climber') and become more global ('they'll think I'm a terrible person'). You can see how this is an example of a number of thinking errors combined, with elements of catastrophising, emotional reasoning and mind reading.

There is a lot of data in this thought, which makes it useful, if unpleasant! First, it outlines how important climbing is to our sense of identity. Second, it suggests that our sense of self-worth is wrapped up in achievement, rather than having broader dimensions such as our personality and personal attributes. Third, it can suggest that important people around us may have inadvertently instilled the idea that it's what you do, not who you are, which is important. It is important to question these assumptions, and figure out, are they true? Do they matter? Do you actually believe this? Do you judge others in the same way? What do you think make a good person?

You can use the technique below to work on the latter assumption, about what makes a good person. Think about all the elements which you feel add up to being a 'good person'. Maybe its kindness, being motivated, being able to cheer people up, doing well at sports and so on. Try to generate a list of all the elements that make up that idea of 'good' personhood. Next, score yourself on each of these elements, using a sliding percentage scale. There is an example below:

Kind   0_____x_____ *100%*

Motivated   0_____x__ *100%*

Cheery   *0_____x_____*   *100%*

Good at sport   *0_____x_____*   *100%*

When you have scored yourself for each element, now return to the idea that you are a terrible person. How would you score yourself now on this assumption, using the same sliding scale? Does this cast doubt on the idea that you are a terrible person? You can do the same for the assumption that you are a terrible climber, or any other judgement you feel about yourself.

SUMMARY

It is normal and natural to worry about the social side of climbing, but it can have a big impact on your own enjoyment and performance. This is mainly due to your attention being focused on what others are thinking, rather than focusing on yourself, your climbing and cues relevant to climbing better. The two main approaches to overcoming this worry involve weakening your belief in the importance of what others think (CBT) and developing an observer position on your thoughts, so they come to feel less powerful (ACT). They both also involve trying out different ways of climbing around other people and collecting data about whether it makes a difference in how you are perceived or not (behavioural experiments). This worry can also show up outside of climbing too, so it will pay to use the techniques both for climbing and other areas of your life where you find yourself facing social worries.

CHAPTER **10**

Other common worries and fears

Of course, fear of falling and worries about being judged are not the only concerns that climbers have. Fear of failure is often talked about in climbing circles, but in my experience it is rarely a fear of failure itself, but more often, a fear of being judged by others during failure which is the problem. This is discussed in the previous chapter. However, what is perhaps more insidious is not so much a fear of failure, but a *preference for sending*. Adult climbers often only attempt climbs that they think they can complete, rather than actively seeking projects that they know they cannot climb *yet*. The downside to this is obvious, in that if you don't try harder climbs or types of moves, rock types or holds that you find difficult, then you won't learn how to do them and it limits improvement. It's reasonable to ask though, why would we do something that works against our own improvement?

I've seen plenty of speculation over the years as to why this might be the case, but in reality, I suspect it will vary slightly from climber to climber. For some people, they simply enjoy the sensation of mastery of a move or climb, and this keeps them motivated, with less motivation and therefore enjoyment present when they try something they can't climb. This would be an approach-type motivation.[1] For other people, being unable to climb something is actively aversive and perhaps at odds with their view of themselves as a climber. This would be an avoidance-type motivation.[2] You may have heard of Carol Dweck's work on mindset,[3] which, although it has a limited research base, suggests that people with a fixed mindset (believing they either can or can't do something) are less likely to persist in new challenges. There is a lot of face validity to this idea, and it's possible to see how this might limit climbing performance. If you think you can't make a certain move, then you are likely to be half-hearted in your attempts, and become quickly discouraged.

STAYING COMFORTABLE

I have noticed that willingness to learn new skills and try new challenges seems to decrease in adults relative to children; children are well used to learning new skills and many (but not all!) are comfortable with the idea of learning and improvement. Perhaps when we adults are competent in many other areas of life, it can be hard to accept the role of being a learner, or of failures being the path to improvement. Sometimes, it's just about the length of time someone has been climbing, perhaps becoming less likely to expand their horizons and comfort zones and address their weaknesses. Being prepared to actively work on weaknesses takes a lot of confidence and resilience, and to be able to do this relies on a sense of psychological safety. If leading or climbing in itself causes you a sense of anxiety most times you climb, then the resources and energy available to deal with that leave little room for expanding your climbing repertoire and training your weaknesses. So energies are best spent increasing the sense of psychological safety first, in order to free up resources to then work on weaknesses.

For some people, they simply avoid the sensation of trying really hard because it feels unpleasant to be at your limit. This would be the equivalent in running of back-to-back sprint sessions, where you try your absolute max every time, and I rarely see climbers doing this. This may be due to feeling anxious about leading, but equally, it can be difficult for people to climb as hard as they can even in low-anxiety situations like top roping or low bouldering. This is likely part of our brain's natural self-preservation instinct, where maximum effort is avoided in order to protect against injury or exhaustion. However, if we never go max out, our body and brain's protective mechanism never gets challenged, we never learn how much we are capable of, and the gap between how hard we are prepared to try and our actual maximum performance stays large.

So, what should you do if you notice you have this reluctance to try routes or problems which you feel might be too hard for you?

1. Try to work out what it is you are avoiding and why?

Does it seem like you can't climb to failure in front of others? Are you too invested in a sense of being competent? Are you too anxious to try anything new? Do you get disheartened easily? Or is it you literally don't know how to hold a sloper for example? Figure out what types of situations, moves, terrain or climbs you avoid and why.

2. Routes – break it down

Rather than being very all or nothing in your assessment of whether you can or can't complete a route, try to work out which portions you can complete, and whether there is a way to complete those sections so that you can try the route. Having the 'give it a go' mindset where you cultivate a curiosity about how much of the route you can complete is more helpful than pre-judging whether you can or can't climb something. If needs be, take a 'get out' kit – a krab or bit of gear you don't mind leaving behind if necessary. Think 'I wonder how high I can get' rather than 'I won't be able to do that, it's too hard for me'.

3. Get used to trying really hard

Aim to have at least one route or problem each session where you give it your absolute max. This should be something you feel safe to try (so if you are not comfortable with leading then use top roping or bouldering). Have several attempts on it (but not too many on a single move, to protect against injury) and score your effort on each attempt on a scale of 0–100%. How close to 100% can you get? It takes time to train your ability to give it your all, and most importantly you will not be able to give it your all unless you feel safe. So working on anxiety around climbing first will pay dividends.

UNHELPFUL EXPECTATIONS

Do you ever find yourself not being able to get up something you think you *should* be able to climb and wondering why? Again, it's not so much a fear of failure in operation here, as having unhelpful expectations in the first place. Whilst having an expectation of success is helpful, and indeed can instil confidence, it can be counterproductive if it causes us to get focused on the wrong things. The wrong focus could be, for example, what other people think rather than how we are climbing perhaps. Or perhaps due to having an expectation of success, we don't give a route enough preparation, concentration and technique attention. Distraction and complacency have slightly different causes and effects, but ultimately they both mean that we are not attending to the here and now of the climb in front of us. Of course, if you are someone who competes a lot or who is an elite climber and there are consequences to not performing at your best, then a fear of actual failure may well be important, but for most recreational climbers, then bombing out in a comp or messing up your redpoint whilst being filmed is not an issue.

Working on developing your focusing and attention skills, and adopting a curious mindset, can help to minimise the impact of expectations on your climbing. Mindfulness skills can be really helpful to enable concentration to be focused on the right things, so that when that mental chatter about what you should and should not be able to do shows up, you can refocus on the task at hand.

Exercise – developing curiosity about your climbing

Spend a few minutes talking about the kind of climbing you like to do, with your climbing partner, or, write down a few paragraphs about it. Talk about what types of rock, moves or lines you find enjoyable, easy or difficult, and the ones you tend to avoid. Notice when your brain is taking a mental shortcut, making judgements about whether you can or can't do something, seeing things in very all-or-nothing terms. Maybe it's something like 'I can't do slopers' or 'I can't climb F7a'; notice the statements you make about your climbing.

Slow down for a moment and notice any related thoughts or feelings that arise. Do you find yourself feeling resigned, frustrated, foolish even about the rules you have for your climbing? Can you approach these 'facts' and 'givens' about your climbing in a different, non-judgemental way? Can you be curious about why these rules have developed? What would happen if you began to explore these ideas you have about your climbing abilities and preferences? Could you, just for one month, begin to test out the ideas you have held as fixed, and see what happens? Try pausing whenever you notice a fixed idea creeping in, even if this is midway up a climb! Try to interrupt your mental short-cutting, and explore the ideas rather than closing down your options. Try asking questions, such as 'I wonder why I find slopers difficult?' or 'how can I find out whether I can climb F7a?' or even 'is there any part of a F7a that I can climb?' or 'what skills do I need to climb F7a?' There are many questions you can ask for any assumptions you make. You can try to brainstorm as many questions as possible for each shortcut you have, and spend some time exploring them both on and off the rock.

REFRAMING UNHELPFUL EXPECTATIONS

It's also important to address some of the thought patterns that can go alongside a lack of focus on the climbing. Noticing when you have thoughts such as 'I should be able to do this' 'I usually manage F6's ok' or even 'this is too hard for me' or 'I can't do this grade' and similar thoughts which predict what you can and can't do is the first step towards altering your mindset. These thought patterns are often so ingrained that we may not even notice them. Of course, they can also be helpful to a degree in making sure that we get our challenge level right by not trying an E7 when we are mainly a HS climber, but holding them too rigidly can mean we either under-challenge ourselves, or give ourselves a hard time when we don't make the grade we had in mind.

These thoughts tend to be at their most insidious when we are around our performance envelope – with climbs which are just above, at or just below or current abilities, and can prevent us taking enough care over some routes, or being so worried we climb badly, or even that we don't give the route or problem a proper go at all. It is the last scenario which is more commonly thought of as a fear of failure, where we try to protect our ego by not giving something our wholehearted effort, but I rarely see climbers who are purely motivated by avoiding bruising their ego! Indeed, their unhelpful expectations often lead to more ego-bruising episodes than would have occurred if they hadn't tried their hardest!

If you notice yourself having these kinds of thoughts, you can ask the following questions;

1. How do I know this?
2. To what degree is this true? (0–100%)
3. Might there be another way to look at this?
4. Is this an accurate appraisal of my abilities vs this challenge?
5. How might my climbing partner see this?

Asking these questions can help pause the mental shortcutting which occurs when we think 'should, must, ought, can't' which tends to lead to 'yes/no' outcomes, and instead helps us to see the nuances required for climbing at our best. In this way, we can start to open up our view of the route or problem, rather than closing down our options into 'can do it/ can't do it'. A good way to do this is to turn some of your thoughts into questions, for example.

'I should be able to do this' > 'I wonder what the best way to climb this is?'

'This is too hard for me' > 'I wonder where the harder sections are and where might be more straightforward?'

'I can't do corners' > 'I wonder which way I'll be facing for this section?'

'The friction is terrible' > 'I wonder how to get the best friction on that section?'

It's important to be clear that turning expectation statements into questions is not about being tentative, but, rather, it's about moving from an all-or-nothing mindset, into a more 'shades of grey' and open mindset. Turning expectation statements into questions begins to open up possibilities on the route, rather than categorising what we see in front of us, and essentially means we are reducing reductionism! We are now in a place where we can experiment and play, with a wider variety of outcomes rather than just send/not send.

FEAR OF FAILURE

If fear of failure in its own right is a thing for you, and you find yourself preferring not to try, than to try something and fail, and it's not because you are worried about what other people think, then you are in the minority! It's worth checking out what it is exactly about failure which bothers you, and using the downward arrow technique we used in previous chapters can help you get to the bottom of your worries about failure.

Some climbers are very attached to outcome and to a sense of mastery, and feelings of incompetence can be very aversive. If this is you, then redefining success and failure is one way of detaching slightly from these thoughts, as is reminding yourself that learning and mastery only comes from repeated 'failures'.

Exercise: What is success to you?

Compare and contrast what you consider the days you climbed at your best, and your most enjoyable days climbing. Are they the same? If they are different, how do they differ? What made them the best or the most enjoyable? How do they map onto your life values and your climbing values? Which did you learn most from and what did you learn? What are your aims with your climbing development? What would you consider a successful climbing experience?

DWELLING ON MISTAKES

Ruminating on mistakes, missed moves or dropped problems to the degree that it inhibits your performance on the next route or problem is another type of worry affecting some climbers. I often see this in younger climbers who are competing, where a mistake on a route means they mess up the next one, because their focus is still on the last route and not what is in front of them. Again, focusing on the task at hand is a good skill to learn, but it can also be useful to have some specific tips and tricks to park the perceived failure until a later time.

I enjoyed hearing about a pole vaulter in the Olympics who, after every jump, made a note about their jump, using a predefined, objective rating scale, and used this to adjust for the next jump. I really like this strategy, as it helps to overcome the tendency to lump performance into either 'good' or 'bad' categories. Noting what went well, even on a dropped problem or route, against predefined criteria (did you use the techniques you set out to use, how was your concentration, did you put enough dynamism into your moves and so on), as well as *what you will do more of next time* (i.e. a positive spin on improvements to be made) can help to shift the focus from mistakes and front-load better performance for the next effort.

You can also use more visual and practical techniques. Have a go at the techniques below.

Exercise: Stamp it out

If you make a mistake and are remaining on the route or problem, imagine yourself squishing it with your foot as you move up, leaving it on the hold it belongs. It can help to give any mistakes a name or image beforehand, especially something comical, to help you detach a little. For example, calling the mistake the 'Ooops' and imagining that word as you squish it with your foot. You can also do this as you fall, imagining the mistake image stamped into the wall or mat as you land.

Exercise: Leave it on the mat

As you come to start your next problem or route, imagine your mistake on the mat, and 'wipe' it off your shoes on it to pin it there. You can pick it up when later for analysis, but for now, imagine yourself pinning it to the mat.

Exercise: Blow it off

If you can imagine your mistake sitting in your hands, then you can blow it off as you would excess chalk. Imagine your mistake blowing out as a puff of particles, and disappearing into the ether. You can do this as you chalk up if you feel self-conscious.

Like any new techniques, you'll need to practise them regularly to embed them in your mind, so you can pull them out of your mental toolkit when you most need them. Remember to practise the transition into them in a controlled practice environment; so, decide on the image for the mistake, make a mistake and practise leading straight into the technique to let go of it.

FEARS RELATED TO SELF-JUDGEMENT

At the heart of some of our climbing concerns and worries can be deep-rooted fears about the sort of person we are. These may not be obvious at first glance, but for example, worries about our performance stemming from worries about being judged may be linked to the concern that we are in some way flawed and will be found out. This is sometimes described as imposter syndrome. It can be broader than just being found wanting however; sometimes climbers may worry about being useless, unlikeable, untalented, a nothing, a nobody. We may have some stories about ourselves that have been circulating in our mind for many, many years, affecting our self-worth and confidence, and screwing with our climbing heads. These stories may have developed out of our upbringing, our life experiences or traumatic events that shape us, and can hang around for a long time afterwards, even when we feel we and our lives have changed. If this sounds familiar, it may be worth investing in some therapy to get to the root of the problems, and guide you in finding new stories to write about yourself.

It can be helpful to think about these stories as passengers on our mind-bus. We carry them with us wherever we go, and sometimes their chatter is louder, sometimes quieter. You might have noticed their words showing up when you are climbing, especially if you are not climbing too well. The exercise below is designed to help you figure out who is on your mind-bus, and to help you get a little perspective on these characters. By externalising them when you draw them out, it helps with getting a little distance from them, so you can see them as separate parts of you.

Exercise: Passengers on the bus (adapted from Acceptance and Commitment Therapy[4])

Imagine you are the driver of a bus, which is going in the direction of your climbing values. The themes, negative thoughts and negative self-stories that show up when we climb can be thought of as passengers on the bus, and we carry them with us wherever we go. They may have been there for a long time, they may have got on more recently after a difficult spell in our lives. Can you give some of these passengers a name, a character? Can you draw them – what do they look like? Who is the noisiest, the biggest, the smallest? What shapes and colours do they have? Are there some unruly and disruptive characters? Are there some helpful passengers too? Who sits where? Who tries to influence you, the driver, the most?

We can't throw these passengers off our mind-bus; we need to learn how to drive in the direction of our values, bringing our passengers along with us. Often, these passengers got on our bus with good intentions – to keep us safe, to make sure we belonged, to help us excel. In your mind's eye, meet and greet each passenger, and acknowledge what their job was at first, even if by now they have overstepped the mark. Thank them for their contribution, and remind them that you are driving the bus. You can even ask them to sit back and enjoy the ride if you like! Imagine yourself driving your mind-bus, towards your climbing values, with your passengers' chatter fading into the background as you focus on your driving, much like you may have done in real life.

Whenever these passengers show up when you are climbing, try to name them, greet them and thank them, then return your focus back to your climbing. For example, 'Hi Judge Dread, thanks for coming, I've got it under control'. This will get easier the more you practise.

FEAR OF RE-INJURY

It's really tricky coming back after an injury. Your mind remembers how hard you used to climb, and your body remembers the pain of an injury. Commonly climbers either apply too much grunt, and are impatient to be back to where they were previously, and run the risk of re-injury; or, they are tentative and protective over their old injury and avoid certain moves and find they are climbing well below their capability. The task therefore is to find a middle ground, where you are able to listen to your body cues and also park your expectations about how hard you used to climb. Thoughts about what we used to be able to do and what we want to do, a sort of flipping forward and back in our mind, distract us away from the here and now and focusing on the climbing, training or rehab in front of us.

a. **Dealing with impatience**

The pressure of expectations are a well-known cause of drop in performance. A certain amount of pressure and we can feel extra motivation, but in situations with factors outside of our control, the pressure becomes unhelpful and counterproductive. Thinking about what factors are in our control can be really helpful at this point, and how quickly we come back from an injury is an outcome we have little control over, but how well we engage with our physio, how we balance training and rest, and the depth of focus on technique to prevent re-injury are all within our control.

Learning mental skills is a great use of injury time, and finding a purpose in the time out can help to stay motivated. Being able to stay focused on the task in hand and on each moment, rather than getting hooked by thoughts about the past or future, is one way to manage impatience. Allowing these thoughts to come and go, and simply observing them rather than engaging them in a mental conversation, can take some of the pressure off.

Equally, understanding that impatience is a close emotional relative of anger, and often about fairness, can be helpful. Have a think about what feels unfair about the injury, and who or what are you really cross with? Sometimes, it may feel unfair, but when we really analyse the situation, we realise we hadn't been paying attention to that niggle in our finger, we hadn't been doing the eccentric exercises someone recommended or we simply hadn't been paying attention to the rock quality. Realising an injury was in some way our fault is somewhat depressing, but is more aligned to the reality of the situation than a feeling of 'it's not fair', and acceptance of reality is a great place to start rehab. It can also help to forgive yourself for any failings which led to the injury, and one way to do this is to write a letter to yourself, in the third person, detailing your forgiveness, and how you will look after your body better in the future.

Exercise: Forgiveness letter

If you find that you are dwelling on feeling cross with yourself for getting injured, perhaps because you feel a sense of self-blame, then take some time to write a letter of forgiveness to yourself. Write it in the third person, as if you were writing to another person, and outline all the factors which led you to the injury. Include any mitigating circumstances, how you feel about the injury, and be sure to write the words 'I forgive you'. You can then use the second part of the letter to detail how you are going to move forwards and make the most of the injury time.

b. **Dealing with being protective of your injury**

What often happens in this scenario is the climber inadvertently tenses up around the area of the old injury in order to protect the injury site, or tenses up on certain moves related to the cause of the old injury. Muscle tension is a common side effect of anxiety, but as part of the anxiety cycle, it can also contribute to anxiety and so we have a vicious circle. Likewise, we may hold our breath as we make a move that we are worried about making, and this contributes to increased anxiety, and may even increase the risk of re-injury or injury elsewhere in the body if we are holding ourselves strangely and not moving freely. So the task is to release any additional and unnecessary muscle tension, breathe freely and then to gradually increase the exposure to the moves which cause you worry.

Climber study: Dave

Dave dislocated his shoulder whilst leading a route at Tremadog. Over the next six months, he dislocated it a further three times in relatively low-key situations, and so stopped climbing. After waiting a year he had an operation to repair a labrum tear. He was diligent about his physio and as soon as he was signed off medically began to climb again. However, he found it really hard to try any move where he was reaching up and out right, the original way he dislocated his shoulder. This hugely limited his climbing, and he began making lots of complex moves to try to compensate for not reaching in that direction.

Observation of Dave noted that he was holding a lot of tension in his body and particularly in his upper body when climbing, prob-ably subconsciously protecting the old injury site. This was limiting the range of his movement and his ability to 'test out' his post-op strength. He worked on using the muscle tense and release exercise to release muscle tension, and developed a routine of breathing out as he reached right. We also encouraged him to stay in the 'out right' posi-tion for increasingly longer times, breathing through any worries or discomfort, in order to build up a bank of shoulder-trust experiences.

You can also use visualisation techniques to help you build confidence in your post-injury body, imagining yourself making moves without difficulty, and with no niggles at the injury site. This is quite helpful prior to starting climbing again, in waking up those dormant neural connections, as well as increasing the sense of self-efficacy. There is more information of imagery use after injury in section 3.

c. **Thoughts about re-injury**

Climbers often report that worries about re-injuring themselves is one of the hardest fears to deal with. Their minds keep returning to thoughts or worries about getting hurt again, and they often get hooked on mentally reassuring themselves that they will be fine. Unfortunately, although this is an intuitive tactic, reassurance is rarely effective and often actually reinforces the anxiety. Mental reassurance functions a bit like the other safety behaviours we discussed previously, in that we are actually trying not to think about the injury worries, but by pushing the thoughts away, they tend to come back stronger. Cutting out the internal reassurance can be one way therefore to actually reduce anxious thoughts. But what to do instead?

We can use the two main models, ACT and CBT, to help deal with thoughts about re-injury. In CBT, we would look to introduce doubt to the idea that we will get injured again, through thinking about how the old injury happened, what rehab work we have done since then and how likely it is to reoccur. Remember that anxiety often makes us see risks more than benefits, and we may need to actively draw our attention to all the positive steps we have taken since the old injury to put ourselves in better shape or to ease back into climbing. You might also find it helpful to draw out a control map of what is under your control (technique, choice of terrain, rehab, etc.) and what is not (slips, slimy holds, etc.) and focus on controlling the controllables. From an ACT perspective, if we are committed to climbing and what it gives us is core to our values, we might want to use ways observing the thoughts rather than engaging with them. Using any of the techniques we use for other fears and anxieties described in chapter 5 will work, helping us to unhook from the anxious thoughts, and instead focus on what is important in the here and now.

d. Reoccurring thoughts about an accident

It's really important to make the distinction between worries about re-injuring ourselves, and repeated and intrusive thoughts about an accident we were involved in or witnessed, as a source of worries about injury. The former is a normal and natural part of coming back after injury, but the latter can signal a more significant underlying issue. Traumatic events such as having a serious fall, being hit by falling rocks or belaying or witnessing someone nearby having a traumatic climbing accident can result in a post-trauma reaction, such as PTSD (post-traumatic stress disorder). In PTSD, symptoms such as reoccurring thoughts and images of the accident (flashbacks), nightmares, irritability and avoidance of accident-related triggers are ongoing (longer than four to six weeks). I've worked with a few climbers where this was the case, and they were unaware that their symptoms were characteristic of PTSD. They had been just forcing themselves to get out climbing again, but suffering quite debilitating anxiety, panic attacks and flashbacks when doing so. PTSD requires specialist help, as after around six weeks, the symptoms are unlikely to resolve by themselves.

There are two main treatments of choice: eye movement desensitisation and reprocessing (EMDR) and trauma-focused CBT, which are both evidence-based ways of treating PTSD. If you are UK-based, it can be difficult to get this treatment on the NHS due to the long waiting times, so if you are looking for treatment privately, look for a clinical psychologist or therapist registered with HCPC or BABCP. Work on processing the trauma first off the rock, and then when you feel ready, the techniques we have already outlined for managing anxiety will help you as you return to climbing.

SUMMARY

Fear of failure, where the climber is worried about failure in its own right and not because of fears of being judged, is not so common. However, having a preference for sending, unhelpful expectations and worries about re-injury are issues many climbers face. A combination of CBT, ACT and mindfulness techniques can be helpful to notice thought processes which close down options, and to open up a more curious mindset, unhooking from thoughts and bringing our focus back to the present moment. If you do find yourself having persistent thoughts about an injury-causing accident, then this needs specialist input and should be resolved first before doing any work around worries about re-injuring yourself.

SECTION 2

Summary

With skills in anxiety management, unhooking from thoughts and reframing unhelpful thoughts and beliefs, you will be on the road to tackling the key psychological issues most climbers face. Falling practice is just one part of this armoury, and should never be the first go-to for climbers. Indeed for some climbers, falling practice as it is commonly carried out is actively unhelpful, making the fear worse, not better. Developing skills in emotion management is not a wasted effort however, even if you don't get as far as falling practice, since emotional control contributes to confidence.

This next section covers the main psychological skills for finessing your climbing performance, and can be tackled by anyone who has been climbing long enough to have the basics in place. These skills have been shown to be helpful not just to climbers, but more broadly in sport. The key is making the skills practice as specific to climbing as possible, which is the focus of section 3.

SECTION 3

Finessing your mental skills

With clear goals in place, and some of the problems in your climbing being more manageable, now you can start to learn some of the skills that top-level athletes use for improving their performance. Of course, it's fine to learn these skills even if you still feel anxious climbing, or even work on these first if, say, working on the fear of falling is too daunting; they will still be helpful but be prepared for them to go out of the window if your anxiety levels shoot up.

The evidence base for the skills in the next chapters is much stronger and comes from sports outside of climbing. Wherever possible here I have adapted them to make the learning exercises more climbing-specific so you can apply them more directly to your practice. Mental skills covered include confidence and self-efficacy, visualisation and imagery, creating conditions for flow, focusing, pre-climb routines and self-talk. These are all skills which can be practised both on and off the rock, so they are ideal for working on during periods where you might be laid off due to injury or, say, the winter training period where you want to lay good foundations ready for summer sending.

CHAPTER **11**

Climbing confidently

Most of my coaching clients want to develop their confidence when climbing and leading. For many that means working on anxiety management, but that's not the only way to develop confidence, and indeed confidence is not necessarily the opposite of anxiety. There's also often a desire to feel confident internally before changing any behaviour, but in reality, if we wait to magically feel more confident, we may be waiting a long time. Confidence is something which can be actively developed by *behaving* differently, and that means doing more than just saying some mantra daily in the mirror! So what is confidence, and how do we develop it through our climbing behaviours?

WHAT IS CONFIDENCE?

Confidence can be described as your belief in your ability to complete a specific task in order to obtain a specific outcome. You might sometimes see the phrase 'self-efficacy', a term first coined by social psychologist Albert Bandura back in the 1970s.[1] It's often described as a *feeling*, but I think this can be unhelpful, since there are specific ways you can *behave to develop* confidence – it's not something you have or don't have, though it might seem that way. It should not be viewed as an all-or-nothing state; we can be confident about certain elements of our performance (for example, our ability to complete a crimpy route) but not about others (our ability to complete a sustained overhanging route for example), though in my experience, climbers rarely remember this at crunch time! Taking control over developing your sense of confidence is an important step, and it's well worth the time to systematically and regularly map out the sources of your confidence, to really imprint them in your mind. Having a confidence book, jar (where you add in all your sources of confidence, each one on a separate piece of paper) or a spreadsheet if that's your cup of tea will help you to note, remember and review your sources, and really help you develop your confidence.

COMPONENTS OF CONFIDENCE

Controllable sources of confidence come from our own previous experiences, vicarious experience (watching similar others doing what we want to do), managing our emotions and verbal persuasion (what we tell ourselves or what others tell us). There are, of course, some people whose personalities include an innate source of confidence, but we are not going to focus on that, since it is not controllable. If you are being coached or are part of a climbing team, then the coaching environment and how you are coached will also have a role to play. But keeping this broad since the majority of climbers don't have a regular coach, we are going to think about the general social environment we find ourselves in.[2]

a. **Previous experience**

We will all have a bank of positive climbing experiences; no matter how often we have wobbles when climbing, we may just have forgotten to foreground them. Negative experiences are much easier to recall and in more detail than the positive, and so these tend to dominate when we think about our climbing experience. We are hardwired to remember difficult or scary experiences in technicolour detail[3] mainly so we can learn from our mistakes and not repeat them, whereas we tend to gloss over things that go well and remember them in general terms.

You can assist your confidence by elaborating your memories when things do go well. Spend a couple of minutes saying out loud or noting down in a book, what went well on a climb. Even if there is nothing much to write home about, was there a single move or decision that you are proud of? Did you figure out a sequence quickly, or get the exact piece of gear for a fiddly crack straight off? Think of this as making deposits in your bank of positive experiences, and try to make them as specific as possible. Think about what you did well, why you did it well and how you did it well.

Exercise: The what, how and why of positive self-feedback

Make a note: What did you do well? Can you write as much detail as possible about what you did well, as if describing it to someone else so they could recreate it? What would another climber see you do?

Next, think about how you did well. What was the process you used to do well? How did you plan or execute the move/sequence/route? What movement, tactical, technical or psychological skills did you use? How would you explain what you did to another climber so they would know what to think about and what they should feel in their bodies?

Finally, write down why you were able to execute that move or sequence well? What did you focus on? How did you move your body to execute it? What mental skills did you use? What worked on this occasion? Why was your success a success?

Many climbers struggle to make a purely positive 'deposit', instead countering what they did well with an immediate self-criticism such as 'I did get the crux but I really faffed with the gear before it'. If this is you, then try to ask yourself instead, what will I do more of next time? This will encourage you to couch your self-analysis in more positive terms, and also will give you a better idea of what to work on next time. So instead of 'I faffed with the gear/don't faff with the gear next time', if you ask yourself 'what will I do more of next time', then the response might be 'take time to feel and look at the gear placement before trying to get a wire in' or even 'look for a more balanced body position before trying to place gear'. The difference now is that you have thought about what to do to rectify the problem, rather than just criticising yourself for having had a problem in the first place. This kind of reframe is much more effective as it's linked to instructional self-talk (see later).

Of course, sometimes in our impatience to improve, we don't take the time to consolidate our climbing and rather than building solid foundations of prior experience, we rush through the grades, barely climbing one or two before moving on to something harder. I see this often with people transitioning from indoor to outdoor sport climbing, or from purely sport climbing into trad, where they lack the experience to even analyse the additional factors present outside the physical difficulty of the climbing, let alone address them. In thinking about our experience, the Johari window[4] is a useful concept. The Johari window in this context refers to our climbing knowledge as a matrix, with the things we know that we know (known knowns), things we know that we don't know (known unknowns), but the bigger risks come from your blind spot (factors unknown to you) and the unpredictable elements (unknown unknowns). Everyone, even elite or experienced climbers, will be subject to the latter two elements, but experience, reflection and analysis will help you to increase the known knowns and the known unknowns and reduce the risk from our blind spots.

Risks are often thought of in purely physical terms (will I injure myself, will this block hold, will my abseil anchor hold?), but mental or psychological risks should not be ignored. Pushing too fast can risk our confidence, and it takes much more time to restore confidence that has been lost than it does to build it gradually in the first place. This is something that coaches need to be aware of when considering how to push on a stage, particularly for younger climbers where they see potential.

b. **Vicarious experience**

This simply means that confidence can be gained by watching someone else do the same route or problem as you suddenly see that it is possible after all. There have been some notable examples of this in recent climbing history. For example, the route Indian Face suddenly saw a flurry of ascents in 2013 (three new ascents in a week[5]), and once one climber breaks a grade barrier, then others will follow. This has been evident in women's climbing, with the numbers of women climbing 8a and above steadily increasing in recent years, as more women see the grade as possible.

However, there is a key ingredient which makes this more likely – you must perceive the other climber to be *like you* in some important ways. Just as beta from a 6-foot-tall male climber is not very helpful if you are a 5ft 2in female climber, watching someone you view as much more experienced or much stronger complete a route does not necessarily translate into increased confidence for you. For coaches, this is important as what you consider similarities between climbers may in fact be perceived as differences from the climbers' perspectives. It does emphasise the importance of climbing with people you perceive to be at a similar standard to yourself. This can be hard if you and your climbing partner are both at very different points in your climbing career, as well as perhaps having different physical attributes, something that can be common with life partners who climb together. I have worked with many climbers whose confidence has been inadvertently destroyed by always climbing with a partner who climbs much harder than they do, and whilst they may get to second some extremely hard routes, continuously feeling like the weaker climber erodes their own confidence over time. A much better strategy is to have slightly different climbing partners for different objectives. If you have time off together with your life partner and want to go climbing, then what kind of climbing would you both enjoy? This can be found by thinking about your climbing values and seeing where they overlap. Saving your try-hard days for someone who is at a similar level as you and who you find inspiring is likely to yield better results – and if this is also your life partner then great.

c. **Managing your emotions**

This is covered in section 2, but in short, knowing we can manage our worries, nerves or fears is a great confidence boost. Just anticipating that we will have a range of emotions to manage when climbing, and having a plan of how to manage them, is way more effective than just hoping fear doesn't show up. Many climbers waste energy wishing they didn't feel scared on the lead, rather than acknowledging that they do have worries, anticipating at what points it will be worst, and developing a plan to deal with it. You will have plenty of experience in other parts of your life in managing difficult feelings – did you ever sit an exam, deliver an important presentation or have to give some awkward or difficult news to someone? What did you learn from the experience? Did you do anything which helped you to get through it despite feeling anxious or dreading it? Take some time to think about strategies which worked for you in other areas of your life, and see if you can apply them to your climbing.

Imagery can be a great way to practise feeling confident at dealing with anxiety-provoking situations. You can practise a route or problem with a psychological crux in your mind's eye, using the skills you learnt in section 2 to successfully manage any feelings that arise, and going on to successfully complete the route despite feelings of nervousness or worry. Do spend time practising your emotional management techniques; they will work only if you can remember how to use them in a sticky spot.

d. **Verbal persuasion**

Perhaps the most used and yet least effective form of building confidence, verbal persuasion refers to what we and others say to ourselves both before and after we climb. Coaches take note – what you say is important. It is not always the best way to build confidence in your climber, but it can be a quick way to destroy your climbers' confidence if you are careless with your words.

For feedback (to ourselves and from others) to be effective, then it needs to have certain attributes. Motivational talk such as 'go on, you can do it' is less effective than instructional self-talk.[6] Instructional self-talk is all about what to do and how to do it, rather than a generic statement about just being able to do it. Likewise with coach feedback, specific statements about *how* a move, problem or route was achieved are far more likely to instil confidence than a simple 'go for it' or 'well done'. Generic praise sounds less convincing than a good analysis of how the climber did well. If you are self-coaching, it's likely that when you really need it, that specific statement is going to elude you, and so think about it on the ground and rehearse some simple statements to use for when the going gets tough. For example, what physical or mental techniques do you want to focus on? What are you good at doing? What do you need to focus on? What skills do you have already in the bank that you can use? If you have a common error you tend to make, then having a corrective self-statement can be a useful way of instilling confidence.

Exercise

Think about the types of techniques you tend to find most tricky, or the ones you find most effective when climbing. Do you need to push more from the feet, use more momentum, be precise in your footwork? Can you say this in two to three words, and write it down as a reminder? Next think about the times when your inner voice tends to become negative and hold you back. Can you use this as a cue to use your instructional self-talk? Could you weave in this talk as part of your climbing routine, for example, every time you have finished clipping, and are about to set off, breathing out and saying your short phrase?

Climber study: Frensi

Frensi happened to see a video of himself climbing and noticed that he was talking to himself the whole time. Turning up the sound, from walking up to the climb, all the way up, he could hear himself muttering countless negative statements, from how hard the climb looked, to how useless he was and how he needed to pull himself together. Taking that video was a revelation as until now, he'd been unaware of how he'd been speaking to himself from the get-go, and how he was berating himself as he climbed. There was no positivity and no self-compassion, and he realised he was being his confidence's own worst enemy.

After addressing some of the self-criticism off the wall using CBT techniques, we designed some simple statements to use whenever he noticed some negative self-talk occurring. Frensi thought about where his technique tended to unravel as he got stressed by using the video analysis, and used these as prompts for helpful climbing techniques and as instructional self-talk. Switching 'come on you ********, just do it' to 'Momentum' and 'hips in' gave him some useful prompts, and rather than trying to suppress his self-talk (which would have just made it rebound and amplify later), he simply used the pre-prepared statements whenever he became aware of muttering to himself. His belayer could also use those words as prompts, and initially, Frensi asked his belayer to help and wrote the words on the back of his forearms to keep them in mind as he climbed until they became second nature.

Instructional self-talk can and should vary according to what you are focusing on at any one time and the demands of the climb in front of you, and so it does require that you take some time to think about what you need for the climb ahead, rather than simply launching up it and hoping for the best. Similarly, coaches can benefit from noticing what they say. Is the feedback to the climber specific and technique-focused, or is it a generic 'well done'? I've observed many coaches, especially early in their career, tend to go overboard on encouragement thinking this is the path to confidence. Whilst it feels positive and encouraging as it is intended to do, the amount of useful feedback the climber can gain is minimal. It also erodes the climbers' own sense of agency. Clear and simple feedback or prompts can be a much more effective way of instilling confidence in the climber, since it encourages the climber to have confidence in *their own skills* rather than simply feeling as though they are pleasing the coach.

e. **Other sources of confidence**

Visualisation can be used to develop confidence, again provided it is used specifically. I'm not a fan of visualising oneself strutting around, winning all the local comps and climbing everything with ease, since unless you really are Jerry Moffat, this is unlikely to be realistic. However, using imagery to imagine yourself dealing confidently with any given untoward scenario on a climb (like a foot slip or gear fumble); spending time mentally rehearsing a project so it feels familiar and doable; and rehearsing the inner sense of confidence through mentally revisiting past successes are all good ways of using imagery to amplify confidence.[7] There are more ideas about using imagery in chapter 13.

Finally, think about the social environment you are in as a climber. Do you surround yourself with people who are positive and encouraging, and who allow you to climb in a way which suits you? Do you have as much control as you would like over your climbing sessions? Do you feel respected by your coach and team? Do you have a good relationship with the people you climb with, or are there jealousies and rivalries? We know that confidence and motivation are linked, and research suggests that motivation is impacted by our sense of control, mastery and connections/relationship quality.[8] The more confident we feel, the more motivated we are to work hard despite setbacks. The social and motivational climate you climb in therefore plays an important role in developing or destroying your confidence. Whilst we are not in control of what others do and say to us, we are in control of whether we decide to stick around or find a new tribe. If the social circles you climb in are not right for you, then treat yourself with respect and get out of there before it destroys your confidence. Climbing participation seems to be increasing exponentially, and there will be other climbers out there who will be a better fit for you.

Exercises

1. *Video yourself climbing. What do you notice yourself saying out loud? What does your belayer say to you? What climbing techniques could you use more often? Can you turn these observations into simple statements as prompts for confidence from you and your belayer? Write these on your water bottle, your arm or on some note cards to review before you climb.*

2. *Coaches – what are the ratios of specific to generic statements, feedback and encouragement you use? How can you help your climber feel confident in their own abilities and strengths by altering what you say?*

3. *Keep a confidence log book or confidence jar. Note down after every climbing session anything you did well (in as specific terms as possible) and also what you will do more of next time. Think about how you executed certain moves (e.g. 'used the momentum from my hips to make a long move'), rather than outcome-based feedback ('got to the top ok'). Be mindful of the tendency to self-criticise (e.g. 'but I didn't close my hand quick enough when I reached the hold and so fell off') and switch this into a more positive and future-behaviour-focused statement ('close the hand quickly on the hold next time; practise drilling this on some dynamic moves').*

SUMMARY

Confidence can be developed and learnt; it's not something you have or don't have. However, we will all have sources of confidence perhaps within or outside our climbing which are currently untapped. Spending time writing down, rehearsing and recalling times where you did succeed is important, particularly if you have had a string of bad days at the crag. Think about your climbing progression – have you consolidated enough, or do you need more time at a lower grade? Think about climbs in a multidimensional way rather than just the grade when planning your climbing, so that you can give yourself opportunities to build confidence slowly. Consider who you tend to climb with and what impact that has on your confidence, and whether you might find it more inspiring to climb with someone similar to you. Finally, rehearsing some simple instructional statements which focus on techniques to use when climbing is likely to be more effective than simply telling yourself to go for it, and coaches also need to be aware of how they use feedback in terms of climber confidence. The chapter on imagery gives some useful tips about how to also use mental rehearsal as a source of confidence.

CHAPTER **12**

Focusing

This chapter is going to cover focusing for climbing, and two related performance phenomena – flow state and choking. Whilst many climbers will be familiar with the term 'flow' and may have experienced it at some points in your climbing career, 'choking' is not a term often used in climbing, though it is well recognised in other sports. Flow state, that feeling of effortless, flowing movement, full absorption in the climb and sense of time distortion, is such a powerful and rewarding feeling, but for many can feel elusive and may only occur a few times over your climbing years. However it can be cultivated with the right conditions and practices. Choking, which is a catastrophic decline in performance, where even simple well-learnt moves become stilted and blocked, may be an experience most often encountered under high stress (e.g. competing or projecting) or high fear (e.g. onsighting trad or highball boulder problems) and may be more familiar to some climbers than flow.

PAYING ATTENTION

At the heart of many problems in climbing lie focusing difficulties. The ability to focus on the correct cues, triggers and stimuli for climbing well, and sustain that focus in the face of internal and external distractions, is crucial. External distractions might include noise, weather conditions, what others around you are doing and so on. Internal distractions would include our own thoughts and feelings which are not directly relevant to the section we are climbing right now. Some climbers also find that switching their attention is tricky, staying stuck on thoughts of a move that went wrong or on the crux which is now behind them, for example.

Our focusing or attentional skills are part of what is called 'executive functions', and they are controlled by the frontal lobe of the brain. Whilst undoubtedly some people find managing their attention a lot easier than others (for example, people who are neurodivergent with conditions such as ADHD can find sustaining focus very difficult), arguably we have all got a lot lazier with managing our attention span in modern life. Smartphone use and scrolling, multitasking at work or filling our minds with low-effort TV or YouTube is unlikely to be helping us hone our focusing skills, though the jury is out as to whether they actively harm our focusing abilities. A related skill, also linked to our executive function and helpful in climbing, is our visual working memory – that ability to hold in mind a sequence of moves. I wonder how often we now practise our ability to hold in mind a visual map, especially since the advent of satnav, Google Maps, and the increased reliance on verbal/language skills over and above practical and visuospatial skills?

There are several theories of attention[1] which attempt to explain how we manage, sustain and switch our focus. I'm not sure that delving into the arguments in the literature is that helpful for most climbers, especially when the research is still not yet conclusive. Instead, I have found using a couple of analogies to be the most helpful way of explaining focus for climbing, and how to hone it.

TUNING YOUR RADIO

Imagine your mind to be an untuned radio, picking up fragments of multiple radio stations – the odd trepidatious thought here 'it looks thin up there', catching sight of a climber on a nearby route there, the sensation in your forearms and accompanying thoughts 'I'm getting pumped out', and so on. Your attention is fleeting and flitting around multiple inputs from your environment and within yourself. For better climbing performance, we need to tune the radio to just one station, fading out distractions and only focusing on climbing-relevant cues.

I think there can also be confusion about what climbing-relevant cues really are. For example, planning and problem-solving where to go next, whether onsighting or redpointing, whilst crucial in its own right, can be a distraction if it happens *whilst you are climbing*. So thoughts about a crux whilst you are 5 metres away are likely to distract from your ability to climb what is right in front of you now. Similarly, though it's helpful to be aware of the level of pump in your arms, most climbers attend to this cue far too early and with too much focus, feeling as though their hands are about to uncurl, and, in doing so, miss a crucial foot placement or simply give up trying. Whilst at some points on our climb we will need to plan a sequence of moves (planning-doing), whilst climbing, we need to only be focused on executing the moves (known within mindfulness as doing-being[2]). It is also better to pay attention to external climbing-relevant cues (like where the holds are!) than internal cues (for example how pumped you feel).[3]

> If we're not careful, it is all too easy to fall into becoming more of a human doing than a human being, and forget who is doing all the doing, and why. (Jon Kabat Zinn)

So our attention needs to be only on things that will help us climb right now. Another word for this is 'affordances' – the opportunities for movement we see ahead of us. So that means getting really interested in the lumps, bumps, textures, knobbles and direction of the holds ahead of us, and sequencing the shapes we will make with our body to get us there.[4]

HOW LONG DO I NEED TO CONCENTRATE FOR?

If you think about outdoor pitched route climbing, then aiming for focused attention for around 30-60 minutes seems like a reasonable goal; if you boulder then your focus time doesn't need to be so long; if you compete, then you are going to need to be skilled at switching focus and integrating downtime with full laser-beam focus. So the first question to ask yourself is, how long can I stay fully focused on the climbing at the moment? Measuring this will give you an indication of where you are now, and also to figure out what is distracting you. Notice whether your mind is distracted by non-climbing-related thoughts, or whether it is habitually planning ahead, or is it engaged in judgements about hold quality, route quality or even your climbing ability? When you place gear or clip into quick draws, do you give this element of climbing your full attention, or are you already racing ahead? Do you tend to focus on the crux and make mistakes low down? Are you easily distracted by noises and other climbers nearby, or can you stay focused? Understanding what, when and how you get distracted is a helpful starting point.

Exercise

Choose a route of medium difficulty for you, not too challenging but not too easy. As you climb, notice every time your attention wandering away from the holds, either getting too far ahead or onto what is going on around you, or thoughts unrelated to climbing (e.g. your to-do list). Whenever you notice an unrelated thought, raise your hand off the wall and/or wave at your belayer. Your belayer can count for you. Afterwards, discuss where your attention was going and notice any themes.

CONCENTRATION EXERCISES

Even if you are someone who struggles with concentration, there is good evidence to suggest that it is a skill which can be learnt and honed.[5] There are some generic exercises which aim to improve concentration, but climbing-specific focusing exercises will give the best yield for your efforts. From studies of elite climbers, we know that having a good visual search strategy, being able to recall a relatively long chain of moves, and focusing on visual cues for climbing are important, so they are all good topics for concentration exercises. For climbers who may get anxious, then keeping the focus on breathing can be steadying and enable them to climb with more focus.

In general, concentration exercises involve paying deliberate attention to specific climbing-related cues, noticing when your attention has wandered, and gently bringing it back to the task in hand. Trying *not* to think about your typical distractions is generally counterproductive, and actively suppressing techniques like thought stopping should be avoided, due to the rebound effect (discussed further in section 2). In trying not to think about something, whilst you may succeed in the very short term, you're likely to get a surge in those thoughts long term. So, the practice point in all these exercises is noticing when your attention has wandered and gently bringing it back, rather than aiming to never have your attention wander in the first place.

VISUAL SEARCH STRATEGY – LASER BEAM/LASER SCANNER

Sanchez et al.[6] identified having a good visual search strategy as key for onsight climbing. If you've ever had the experience of missing a crucial hold whilst you struggle to get a piece of gear in, only to find it as soon as you are safely clipped, you'll know how frustrating it can be! Exercises to try include switching your gaze from a single point on the rock (laser beam) to sweeping the rock in a systematic way, like a laser scanner, with a softer gaze. Expanding the gaze to as wide as possible also has the benefit of being calming for anxiety, since when we get stressed, we tend to narrow our gaze, or look around wildly almost without seeing (hypervigilance). Try working clockwise, or by quadrant, as a practice of scanning for possible holds. Practise the switch from a wide gaze to a narrow and focused gaze; sometimes we need to keep our eye firmly on a hold to make it happen (accuracy), and other times we need to look for possibilities for movement outside the obvious (wide gaze).

MINDFUL BREATHING

Focusing on the breath has several helpful qualities. First, for most people it is calming and grounding, which is beneficial if you find you get anxious when climbing. Second, it provides a useful cue for concentration and focus, and since the breath is always there, we always have a reminder for paying attention. Third, for some climbers who get overly analytical with their climbing and find themselves overthinking, focusing on the breath can be a way of 'getting out of their body's way' and allowing the body to climb without over-analysing every move.

The technique is simple. Without trying to change anything, simply follow the breath as it enters and leaves the body. You can pay attention to elements such as the feel in the nostrils, the sensation of the lungs or ribs expanding, the feel of the air leaving your mouth and so on. The temptation with mindful breathing is to start to alter your breathing pattern, or find that judgements about your breathing may creep in (e.g. 'I'm breathing too fast'), or simply due to its automatic nature, you may find your mind wandering. I have observed for some people that it can also make them feel breathless, and if they have had breathing problems in the past (e.g. asthmatic), then this exercise may be anxiety-provoking. If this is the case, then switch to a different concentration exercise, or focus on actively using diaphragmatic breathing (see section 2).

The best way to start mindful breathing is lying down, or sitting comfortably. You can then progress to using it whilst walking, and then on an easy route. As you find your concentration improving, you can gradually increase the difficulty of the climb as you practise. On difficult routes or problems, you may find that you have an *awareness* of the breath, rather than out and out concentration, as you will be also paying attention to the moves you need to make, but this is fine and a good sign that you are in the moment.

MINDFUL SEEING

For me, this is the most helpful focusing exercise for climbers. This is where you pay attention to the sensory experience of the piece of rock in front of you. Try to notice the colours, shapes, textures and feel of the rock, and become fully absorbed in it. The idea is to take in the sensory or perceptual input, without judgement (so dispensing with judgements such as 'That's too small to hold' 'my foot will slip off that'). It may help to imagine you are an alien from outer space and have never seen this type of rock before. What can you notice about it? Try to let go of preconceived ideas and simply see and feel the rock.

The aim behind this exercise is obviously to try focusing skills, but also it should start to help you to see more possibilities for movement in the rock, a skill linked to more creative problem-solving (see chapter 14). You can try this anywhere, by carrying around a small pebble or piece of rock; but you can also use this exercise indoors (arguably more distracting due to the huge coloured holds!), at the foot of the crag, and then as you begin to move on easy routes or problems. Many climbers also report they find this quite calming and grounding when used for short sections on hard or stressful routes.

CUE WORDS FOR FOCUSING

Using cue words for focusing (e.g. 'focus'!) can be helpful, but not if used in a vacuum. You will need to specifically link them to times when you have been very focused. So, that could mean spending time specifically recalling a climb where you were fully in the moment, and recreating those feelings in your mind and body, and pairing that with your cue word. Or, it could be trying the exercises listed above and pairing them with your focusing word. Either way, just telling yourself to focus on a climb is unlikely to do the trick, unless you have practised the technique beforehand and know what focusing feels like. It is also important to be clear about what you are focusing on. Without having practised the link to giving your attention to climbing-related cues, simply telling yourself to focus can sometimes lead to an internal conversation or untoward focusing on thoughts, rather than the affordances in front of you.

FLOW

'Flow' is a term coined by Mihalyi Csikszentmihalyi.[7] It has a long definition; referring to an altered state of consciousness, where there is absolute focus and alertness, on a challenge at exactly the right level. During flow, the passage of time can feel both fast and slow, and our actions feel effortless and almost without conscious thought, and all distractions fade into the background. If you've experienced flow, you'll know that feeling and likely want to recreate it, as often that's our best climbing performance. However, if you've never experienced it climbing, it is possible you have experienced something similar; perhaps lost in a book, playing or listening to an intense piece of music, or even when meditating. For many climbers, they may feel their flow experience happened by accident, but it is possible to create the conditions needed for flow to happen, which make it much more likely to occur. Skills need to be well practised so it's less likely to happen to you early on in your climbing career, though later on our expectations of what we should be able to climb can also hinder our ability to experience flow.

EXERCISES TO MAKE FLOW MORE LIKELY TO HAPPEN

Recent research has shown close similarities in the brain activation of people who are experienced meditators and those experiencing the flow state, so this provides one clue as to how to improve your chances of experiencing flow.[8] Learning how to meditate will pay many dividends for your climbing, both in terms of improved focus, increased likelihood of experiencing flow, and also in terms of dampening down the impacts of anxiety on your climbing. Many climbers I have worked with find it hard to practise sitting meditations, but do find moving meditation easier and arguably this is of closer practical use for climbing.

SILENT CLIMBING AND CONTINUOUS MOVEMENT PRACTICES

Exercises which fully absorb you in the movement, in an environment which feels safe to you, can be very helpful for focusing fully on actions and perceptions.

Exercise: Silent climbing

Try climbing without making any noise – silent feet, no brushes of clothing on the wall, making your movements smooth and controlled. This can be done traversing on the bouldering wall, top roping or leading something easy enough that you feel confident to 'forget' about the leading element whilst performing the exercise to start with.

Exercise: Continuous movement practices

Rather like flow sequences in yoga, where movements are repeated and linked and merged into each other, climbing continuously without pause or hesitation can heighten focus and flow. Typically we might climb in short sequences, with a short gap in between as we plan out the next pattern of moves, but in this exercise the aim is to eliminate the gap and simply keep moving. Naturally this is easier on easier routes or climbs, so do start there, but as the routes get harder, you should find you are allowing your body to climb rather than trying to pre-plan and control every movement. So the goal is not perfect climbing, but rather to create a sense of continuous and almost automatic but focused climbing. If you are bouldering, you can also try this exercise by climbing in circles on a piece of wall, rather than going up and down which can lead to pausing as you reverse.

HITTING THE SWEET SPOT

We can think of our levels of internal activation or arousal as a curve, with optimal performance at the top of that curve.[9] Some of us will be easily activated and experience a quick uptick in internal arousal, and some of us are much more of a slow burn. We may also start off on different days with different levels of internal arousal, depending on what is going on in our life at that time – more stress can lead to higher levels of internal arousal. And if you are someone who has had a tough start in life, then your nervous system will be far more reactive and harder to soothe and settle than for someone who has experienced a loving and consistent upbringing.

Everyone is different, which means having a sense of your own levels of internal arousal/stress can be helpful to determine what you need to do to hit that sweet spot for your best climbing. Most climbers I have worked with need to soothe and settle themselves rather than to psyche up; in 15 years of this work only two climbers have needed to activate themselves and psyche up! So learning how to settle your systems down is usually the most useful thing to learn, especially as once you start to climb, you will generally create greater levels of activation. The harder the challenge or the trickier the lead, the greater the activation as you climb, so you will need to account for that in finding your optimum start levels. This is covered in more detail in section 2.

PRE-CLIMB ROUTINES

One way many athletes use to get themselves into the zone is by the use of pre-climb routines. Using a short, two to three action sequence directly before you climb as the last thing you do before you leave the ground and after your safety check, can be beneficial in many ways. First, it provides predictable cues for climbing and performance, a signal to your brain and body to 'get ready'. Second, it links training and sending, bringing the relaxation from training into sending, but also the skills and practices. Third, it can be a way of getting into the right arousal level and a cue to focus. It can take some time to hit on the right routine for you, but when you have something you are happy with that gets you into the right frame of mind, be sure to use it every time you climb. Think of Jonny Wilkinson's actions before kicking a penalty, or Serena Williams's way of bouncing the ball before each serve.

Exercise: Developing your pre-climb routine

Things to consider:

Do you need to be calmer or more psyched?

Are there any performance blockers you need to counteract? (e.g. tending to hold your breath or overgrip for example, where you might want to breathe out fully as part of your routine or shake out)

Can you perform this action every time you climb?

What cue words might help you to use in your mind

Write out a short, two to three action sequence that you can use every time, just before you leave the floor.

Climber Study: Sarah

Sara wanted to lead Comes the Dervish for a while. She had seconded it a few times and knew it was within her capabilities but had always felt nervous about giving it a go. We worked on knowing where she was on her arousal-performance curve, and she developed a routine to use before she climbed which included taking a proud posture (which she associated with confidence and capability), closing her eyes for a moment as she breathed fully out (which she associated with blowing out other thoughts) and then using the cue word 'climb' as she opened her eyes and setting off immediately. She also worked on using mindful breathing at home in between sessions and whilst on the wall when warming up.

On the day she sent it, she warmed up on a couple of routes and used her mindful breathing whilst seconding. She hadn't intended to send it that day, but it just felt like the right day and when the thought of leading Comes the Dervish popped into her head, she went with it without delay. As she got herself racked up, she and her belayer stayed quiet, she gave each racking movement full focus, and, then after her safety checks, stepped into her pre-climb routine. As she breathed out and opened her eyes, she felt like she was in the zone and began to climb. Afterwards, she reported that the climb had just flowed, and she had been unaware of the noise from a group completing an abseil in the quarry nearby, and that she felt as though she had been in the climb for both minutes and hours, loving every movement.

WAYS TO MAKE FLOW MORE LIKELY TO HAPPEN WHEN YOU ARE ACTUALLY CLIMBING

1. Choose a climb because you really want to climb it and not for any sense of 'should' or to please someone else (an autotelic experience[10]).
2. Choose a route which is the right mix of doable and challenging. Arguably, this is the hardest part of setting the right conditions!
3. Spend some time getting yourself into the right level of arousal, whether by psyching up or psyching down (depending on your personality type), meditating and warming up thoroughly with full concentration.
4. Mentally leave any distractions behind. Put your full focus onto the movements in front of you.
5. Find the right pace and be curious and open to the experience ahead of you.
6. Don't try to force it! Flow will happen or not, and if your focus is on trying to create flow, it won't be fully on the climb itself.
7. See the gear placements and clips as part of the movements you need to focus on rather than being separate in some way.

PERFORMANCE BLOCKS: CHOKING UNDER PRESSURE, THE YIPS AND BAULKING

Climbers do experience performance blocks, but we don't tend to use the same terms that you tend to see in the general sport psychology world so some of these labels might be unfamiliar to you. Choking is where there is a sudden and catastrophic decline in performance, for example, where a golfer fails to hit a straightforward putt, usually in high-stress/high-stakes situations and is thought to be due to anxiety-related overthinking. The yips is another related performance block, usually used to describe a very physical response, such as involuntary twitch, jerk or muscular shake, often without a conscious awareness of anxiety. Archers might describe their muscles suddenly twitching outside of their conscious control, messing up their shot. Baulking can feel like it's physically impossible to complete a move, even when it's well practised. An example might be a gymnast taking a run-up for a complex vault, and suddenly finding themselves only executing a simple vault or stopping altogether. Other terms you might see include 'lost move syndrome', and, more recently due to Simone Biles' Olympic experience, 'the twisties'. These phenomena are probably related, still poorly understood and rarely talked about in climbing.

I have certainly observed these kinds of issues happen to climbers. What we might see is a total regression in movement, similar to what happens when someone is very fearful, but also there can be a failure to execute even well-drilled movements, such as clipping or fumbling gear, with a kind of physical 'stutter' present which prevents the movement. I suspect that what some redpointers describe as a fear of failure is actually a performance block under pressure, where the well-rehearsed moves of a sport climb suddenly seem impossible to execute, or your muscle efforts inexplicably fall short, just as you make your send attempt.

There are two main theories of choking, but both relate to performance anxiety. One is that the athlete is distracted by irrelevant stimuli, and the other is that the athlete becomes hyperfocused on avoiding failure. Either way, a well-learnt skill suddenly seems to disappear or deteriorate. Worries about social judgement and criticism may dominate, and the athlete begins to focus more on the risks of not completing the skill than on the cues and focus needed for the skill.

For climbers who have been practising a route for many sessions and feel they have all the moves dialled, ready to try for the send, then being too attached to the outcome (sending the route) can take over the mind with disastrous consequences. Rushing 'easy' sections, fluffing previously nailed moves, hesitating over sequences, climbing tentatively and many other performance errors can creep in, leading to huge frustration, and often with one mistake leading to another.

In terms of the yips, it is thought that the yips are more likely to occur in extremely well-practised athletes, with higher levels of concentration and tension[11] – maybe being overly focused here might be the culprit. 'Baulking' ('balking') is a relatively new term and appears to be a combination of both choking and the yips, and manifests as the body almost refusing to execute certain moves or sequences even if the mind is willing. In all likelihood, the mind is protecting the body in some way, preventing it from making moves where perhaps there is high possibility of injury or where there may be some traumatic memories, or a previous psychological injury. It's likely that in both the yips and baulking, there may be an underlying trauma (either physical or psychological) which is creating the performance block. In these instances, it is best to seek professional help with the underlying trauma first, rather than continuing to try to resolve it alone.

For all these mental blocks, it is likely that attentional focus plays a role. We need to attend to the right cues, at the right time, with just the right amount of focus and arousal, without holding on too tightly to controlling every element of movement. At some point, you need to trust your body to get on with the job it's been trained to do; micromanaging your movements is likely to inhibit them when you are a well-practised climber. We have all been through the stage of learning a new skill where you have to exert conscious control over your body in order to get it dialled; over time, you just need to cue your muscles and your body will execute that dropped knee or gaston without you needing to arrange every muscle fibre into exactly the right place. Performance blocks may signal a lack of trust in our body's ability to climb, perhaps because the stakes suddenly appear higher. They can have a huge knock-on impact on confidence, but it is important to remember that even if it feels that way, the skills you had are not lost, and it is possible to recover them.

So what can we do about blocks?

1. Practise non-attachment to outcomes; focus on process
2. Stay in the moment and focus on climbing-relevant external cues
3. Learn how to recover and reset after a mistake
4. Examine your motivations – who are you doing this for?
5. Use a pre-performance routine to hit your sweet spot
6. Practise, but don't micromanage!
7. Learn to manage your anxiety so you are less distracted by worry and fear

SUMMARY

Learning how to focus and sustain your concentration whilst climbing is possible, even if you are someone who finds it tricky to concentrate in other areas of your life! Many performance problems can be traced back to getting distracted, often by internal distractions such as thoughts or feelings, judgements or over-analysing. Practising climbing-specific concentration exercises which get you absorbed in the movement actions and affordances ahead of you, and will make a flow experience more likely. They will also make catastrophic declines in performance like choking or the yips less likely to happen.

CHAPTER **13**

Imagery and visualisation

This will be a familiar topic to many climbers, but in my experience, use of imagery and visualisation can often be improved, and/or its use can be broadened out to improve the effectiveness and 'reach' of imagery skills. Many climbers will use imagery as part of problem-solving or planning a sequence, but it can also be used as a way of instilling confidence, of imagining how to rectify a mistake or wobbly moment, or to help return to climbing after an injury. This chapter will cover one main framework for good imagery and visualisation practice, and different ways to utilise imagery within your climbing.

HOW DOES IMAGERY WORK?

The reason imagery is so useful is that it activates the same areas in your brain as you would use when actually climbing[1] – parts of the motor cortex – and so it provides an opportunity to 'climb' without taxing the muscles and leaving the ground! It also enables us to try out moves mentally in our imagination, to see if they work, to rehearse them and to learn a sequence so we can call it readily to mind when needed. As such, it is an invaluable skill for climbers.

It is important to note that around 2–5% of people are unable to visualise or see in their minds, a condition called Aphantasia,[2] and so these exercises will require significant adaptation. However, it is still possible to work around this by using other sensory modalities such as body movements/shapes, and some people may believe they cannot use imagery when in fact they simply haven't practised it enough.

GETTING STARTED WITH IMAGERY

If you have never used imagery before then a good way to get started is by playing the climbing game, add a move. This requires you to memorise an ever-increasing sequence of moves, and provides good opportunities for mental rehearsal. Another good way is to simply try to recall how you climbed a short sequence of, say, three moves, and then gradually increase the length of the sequence. You can also try to reverse a short sequence of moves in exactly the same way as you went up it, to improve your memory for a sequence.

Exercise: Add a move

Best played with a small group, pick the starting holds for a section of the climbing wall, and take it in turns to make one hand or foot move each. You can go up, down, left or right at any time. It pays to be savvy and make moves that emphasise others' weakness – for example, if you are shorter climber, now's the time to have your revenge on the taller climbers, by making very scrunched up moves or matching hands on small holds! You will need to memorise increasingly longer sequences, and if you forget the sequence, then you are out of the game.

The tricky part is moving from the memory of a sequence into predicting what a sequence might be and imagining that without having actually climbed it yet. One way to do this is to try to think about the whole body shapes you will need to make. Often inexperienced climbers will focus on the handholds only or footholds separately to the handholds, whereas thinking about the whole body shape will give you a sense of where all your body needs to be. You could try imagining yourself climbing a short sequence, describe that to your climbing partner, then have your climbing partner video you on the sequence. Play back the video – did you climb the way you thought you would? Watching yourself on video is a good way to gather data about the typical way you climb that will help you 'see yourself' in your mind's eye during imagery; however it will also highlight any technique faults you might like to correct!

There is also the factor of experience here, in that the more climbing experience you have, and particularly at a certain climbing venue or rock type, the easier you will find it to predict how to climb that sequence. A new rock type can often throw climbers – if you've been to Fontainebleau, then think of your first visit and having to get your head around the compression moves for example. The broader and more varied your practice, then the bigger the bank of your internal memory for moves and sequences, and the easier you will find it to call to mind imagery for climbing.

THE PETTLEP FRAMEWORK

PETTLEP[3] is an acronym used to describe the key elements for successful visualisation: Physical, Environment, Task, Timing, Learning, Emotion, Perspective.

Physical – imagery should be a physical process with external and internal cues which mimic the actual climbing experience. Be in your climbing clothes, shoes and harness with your rack and rope on, and think about the physical sensations associated with climbing – chalk on your hands, the feel of the rock and the movements your body will make, rather than just what you might see in your mind's eye. You may have seen the video of Adam Ondra getting into some unusual positions lying on the floor, with his physio actively helping him to enhance his imagery and strength in those crucial positions, prior to sending the route *Silence*.[4] This is a great example of using imagery to its fullest extent, and something you can imitate for your own projects.

Environment – ideally, perform your imagery at the crag or wall, or, if this is not possible, then have pictures or videos to help site you there. Think about the feel of the weather conditions on your body, the sounds you might hear and so on. Research shows that the imagery is most effective when you add in cues for the environment, so for a sea cliff route for example, you might want to record seagulls squawking as background noise whilst you imagine yourself climbing the route!

Task – this is the actual task in hand, so the sequence, problem or route you are practising for. Accurately remembering a whole route is hard, so you might want to write down all the elements and record yourself talking through the route, giving as much detail as you need to 'complete' the moves, and then play it back to yourself whilst you go through it in your mind's eye. Remember to include imagery of you placing gear or clipping into quickdraws as part of the task, rather than thinking of these as separate entities. You need a sense of the whole experience ideally.

Timing – the imagery should take as long as it would in real time; however, it may sometimes be useful to 'slow-mo' some sections to correct any errors or to really embed tricky moves. A common problem with imagery is to speed through it too quickly mentally or skip over easy sections, so make sure you don't fall into this trap. You are aiming for accuracy in all elements of the mental representation.

Learning – your imagery script will need to be adapted as you become stronger, fitter or you develop a new sequence, or to incorporate any learning during actual climbing if, for example, you are unable to see a particular section prior to climbing it.

Emotion – include realistic emotions in your imagery. If you do get tense when climbing, then including that sense of nerves can be helpful, as well as also including how you resolve those worries, rather than simply imagining yourself to be calm throughout. Realistic imagery would include heightened arousal at the crux, as well as sense of dampening down that arousal and powering through, with the sense of confidence perhaps from placing that bomber nut beforehand. This way, whatever happens emotionally during your send, you won't be thrown, because you have already practised the resolution beforehand.

Perspective – there has been much debate about whether taking an internal or external perspective is best for imagery; however, many people already have an established preference for one or the other and trying to change it can be too difficult. Seeing the imagery as if through your own eyes, rather than from the perspective of an external observer, is thought to be better, as that is how you will actually view the route when you climb. But if you can only make the imagery work for you as if you were viewing a video of yourself, then go with that rather than trying to change.

Whilst this framework can seem complex for simple rehearsal of a sequence before you jump on a problem or route, this depth of imagery really comes into its own is for building confidence and increasing your chances of success for a route in your stretch zone and where you are uncertain of whether it is send-able or not. Holding this framework in mind will help give a richness to the imagery which will make it more effective, and, if you can, use the framework to pre-record a script with all the prompts to use for rehearsal in between attempts.[5]

USES OF IMAGERY, VISUALISATION AND MENTAL REHEARSAL

If you are only currently using imagery to plan your next few moves, then you are missing out! Imagery can be used for:

1. Reading a section of a route when onsighting
2. Problem-solving for a better solution to a challenging sequence
3. Increasing your confidence in the ability to send a route or problem
4. Route rehearsal during rest periods or when conditions are unfavourable
5. Memorising a route
6. Increasing confidence in managing emotions during a lead climb
7. Keeping climbing mentally activated during recovery from injury
8. Managing expectations following injury
9. Imagery for improving healing post-injury
10. Embedding a particularly tricky move where you need to focus hard on particular elements to make the move work

How many of these do you currently use? Where do you think you might benefit from expanding your use of imagery and mental rehearsal? Chances are, imagery is an untapped resource for your climbing, and if you can include its use more often, it will have a beneficial effect on your climbing.

PROBLEMS WITH IMAGERY

For imagery use to be effective, try to avoid falling into these common traps;

1. Fast-forwarding through the easy sections
2. Getting distracted by external stimuli during mental rehearsal and going 'off script'

3. Getting distracted by thoughts/images about falling, etc. during mental rehearsal (internal stimuli) and not resolving them
4. Only using imagery for hard routes and not practising regularly enough
5. Confusing affirmations with imagery

I'm not a huge fan of imagining yourself just at the point of success, be that topping out on your hardest onsight, or winning a competition. Focusing on the end point or the outcome for your visualisation doesn't give you many clues as to how you are going to get there – there is no process map for you to follow, just the end dream which is likely to be outside of your control. For visualisation to be effective, then it should focus on the elements which are in your control – that is, how you climb, how you manage your emotions, how you problem solve, etc. You cannot control whether you win a competition, as it depends on the performance of your fellow competitors as well as on yourself. And for your hardest climb yet – the top out will follow naturally if you have prepared yourself really well for each move and linking the sequences. It may help your confidence to imagine yourself on the top or on the podium, but unless there is a solid foundation to that image, then the sense of confidence may be short-lived and feel a bit fake.

Climber study – Hardeep

Hardeep was stuck at leading F6b+ and really wanted to progress. During the assessment, when I asked him about what strategies he used to improve his chances of success, he told me he often tried to use imagery but was unable to see himself climbing in his mind's eye. After some discussion, we realised that he did not use any mental visualisation in other areas of his life either, and in all likelihood this meant that he was not able to do so. This really got in the way of his ability to read routes and because of this, he tended to prefer redpointing to onsighting. Hardeep also really hated to mess up sequences, feeling like he was wasting energy.

After some reframing work to help him be more accepting of his difficulty with visualisation, and encouraging him to see messing up sequences as a way of becoming more creative in problem-solving and helping his fitness (he could cling on for a really long time!), we spent some time working out what senses he could use to map out a route in his mind. He found that he could use body movements and cue words to figure out a sequence, as that was how he tended to remember routes when he was redpointing.

The main practices we worked on were trying to increase the number of different ways he solved a sequence problem during redpoint attempts; going with whatever sequence he had, even if he thought it was a mess; and drawing out on a piece of paper the body movements he needed to make, along with cue words. He also began to try this technique on easier onsight climbs with more obvious sequences, trying to predict in advance what the pattern might be, and then moving his body through the sequence whilst looking at the rock whilst on the ground. Hardeep quickly cracked his F6B+ ceiling, and began to enjoy onsighting a bit more.

IMAGERY AS PART OF RECOVERY FROM INJURY

Using imagery as part of your repertoire for recovery has been shown to decrease time to recover and improve feelings of confidence in readiness to return to sport.[6] The mind–body connection is strong and bidirectional, so you can use imagery to enhance your recovery in a number of different ways. Whilst all this may sound a bit far-fetched, there are a good number of research studies showing that imagery can be effective in promoting recovery.

a. **Imagery for promoting healing**

Research from a number of different health conditions, from cancer to sports injuries, suggests that imagining the body healing can have a beneficial impact on recovery and improve outcomes. Whilst the exact mechanism is unclear, we know that the mind–body link can be harnessed to improve outcomes for both body and mind. At the very least, using imagery is likely to feel relaxing (and dampening down the stress response is good for the immune system), to allow you to feel more in control of the outcome, and will at least give you something to do whilst in recovery.

For effective healing imagery, focusing on increasing blood flow to the affected area, imagery for pain relief, and visualising the immune system repairing have all been used in various studies for different conditions, and tend to be associated with decreased distress about being injured. We know that stress has a negative impact on immune function and healing, and so anything that can promote psychological wellbeing and reduce distress will help your recovery.

For, say, a finger or ankle injury where there is swelling, the sensation of swelling can be incorporated into the imagery, where the mental images of the swelling can be 'magnified' to imagine cells of the immune system rushing to the affected area and removing any torn tissue, and muscle fibres or ligament fibres rebuilding themselves. For a bone break, and especially where you have seen the X-ray, you can use the image of the X-ray as a cue in the visualisation, imagining the bone knitting together again cleanly.

b. **Imagery for pain relief**

You will need to consider the characteristics of the pain you are feeling. Does the injury feel hot, burning, sharp pains, constricted, etc.? Incorporating this into the imagery and finding a counter image to soothe the pain can be helpful, as well as weaving in images of a safe or relaxing place. For example, in working with someone with headaches post–head injury, who experienced them as hot and pulsating, we used the image of floating in a natural rock pool (cool not cold!) overlooking the sea (to incorporate the pulsation) at sunset for dimmer light, and bathing the back of the head in the cool pool of water. Pain models emphasise the dominant role of the brain in our experience of pain;[7] that is to say, pain is not just determined by what is happening in our body at an injury site. Our brain interprets and modulates the signals received from our body, and we can use this attribute to improve our management of pain.

If you are having physio as part of your recovery, then this can also be a painful process. Using imagery to help view this pain as positive and helpful can help you to deal with the pain of rehab, as well as promoting healing. Hypnobirthing provides a great example of how to use the mind to manage the experience of pain by the use of positive suggestions coupled with physical and psychological pain relief. If this area interests you, then there are some good academic texts[8] as well as audio scripts available.[9]

VISUALISATION FOR IMPROVING CONFIDENCE WHEN RETURNING TO CLIMBING

Often the hardest part of recovering from a serious injury is having confidence again in the injured body part. For example, after having had a shoulder repair for a labrum tear, feeling confident to hang on that arm again, even though you have had the all clear from the physio or surgeon, can be a huge mind game. Visualising yourself successfully using your injured shoulder, for example, before actually climbing on it will begin to both prepare the shoulder/body part for being used in climbing, and prepare your mind for overcoming those feelings of trepidation. You could build up to imagining yourself making the same moves as those that caused the injury in the first place, but this time changing the ending, so that the shoulder, finger, etc. feel strong, healed and even improved post-surgery/-recovery.

IMAGERY FOR THE WHAT-IFS

If you find yourself plagued by 'what if…?' thoughts, then imagery can be useful to help you work through all eventualities, with successful problem-solving strategies. Think about all the things you worry about that might go wrong – a nut pinging out as you climb upwards, a foot slip, not being able to complete the crux. Write down all these what-ifs, and develop a plan to combat them if they occur. Now, using the PETTLEP framework, imagine the what-if scenario happening, and imagine yourself dealing with it as you have written down. Be sure to include the emotional component, as well as completing your problem-solving in a confident way. Rehearsing these feared scenarios will give you the confidence to tackle anything that the climb throws at you.

SUMMARY

If you are only using mental rehearsal to plan how you are going to climb, then you are not making full use of the advantages visualisation can give you. Try to increase the repertoire of imagery skills by using the PETTLEP model, and broaden out its use to confidence building, managing difficult situations or emotions on a route, and for recovering from an injury. If you are struggling to use imagery at all, consider whether you can use it in other areas of your life (do you have a visual imagination) and if not, then you may need to think of different ways of imagining a route. If you are able to use imagery elsewhere, then it's likely a matter of climbing-specific practice, and so start by mentally rehearsing moves you have already completed or seen others complete, before progressing to predicting or visualising moves you haven't yet tried out.

CHAPTER 14

Being adaptable

Problem-solving and movement creativity

It's beyond the scope of this book to go too much into the mental side of movement skills. To be a good climber, you need to have well-learnt movement patterns and be able to apply them to creatively solve the movement problems in front of you. Building up a broad repertoire of movement patterns is important, but then so is their application according to the constraints of the route or problem in front of you. Here there can be an interaction with confidence – if you lack confidence, you are likely to be more conservative in your use of movement patterns, and stick to the same tried and tested movements, perhaps avoiding entirely routes that, say, have smears or slopers on them. This may even extend to avoiding certain rock types entirely.

However, this is a mistake long term, since by avoiding certain moves, styles or rock types, you are limiting your climbing repertoire and reducing your prospects of being adaptable and creative. Staying in your comfort zone does not pay dividends. The broader your climbing practices are, the more likely you are to be able to come up with the right moves at the right time when you want to push your grade.[1] This chapter is designed to give you some ideas for how to develop that mental flexibility and creativity in your climbing. The book *Climbing Games*[2] will also give you some more ideas for working on each of the elements below.

IMPROVING SPEED

The idea with the exercises below is to get comfortable with varying your pace, but also to learn to speed up your responses. This is as much a mental thing as a physical thing, so you are working on being creative with the speed of your movements, and being able to adjust according to the situation in front of you. It's also a helpful way to learn to trust your body to know what to do, when your conscious mind can't control the outcomes because you are going at speed!

Try:

- the speed wall at the gym – can you beat your time/your climbing partner's time?
- timing each other on a well-learnt route on top rope – how fast can you go?
- having your partner tap the next hold you need to use – how quickly can you respond?
- fast-slow-fast-slow – between panels or clips if outdoors, can you climb as fast as possible, then as slowly as possible, then fast again and so on?

IMPROVING ACCURACY

Ideally we want to hit every hand and foothold in exactly the best spot to make the most use of what it offers. Whilst it's kind of obvious in terms of footwork when this doesn't happen – the sound of feet slapping around – it's perhaps more subtle for hands. Often we find ourselves adjusting and readjusting our grip once we have a hold, wasting valuable energy and time. Keep the difficulty easy on these exercises but aim to be very precise about where you hit each hold.

- first touch – try not to adjust on any particular hold, just use it as you first grasp/foot it
- accurate feet – try aiming for a particular spot on a hold or the wall at increasing distances from your body
- aiming to hit increasingly small foot- or handholds at a distance, or marking out-of-bounds areas on holds and trying not to touch them

CREATIVE PROBLEM-SOLVING

We all have preferred ways of moving or using holds, but it pays to get out of your comfort zone and deliberately practise alternative ways of moving and climbing. Try the following exercises to help shake things up a little.

- add a move – best played with a group of friends of diverse shapes and heights! Take it in turns to add a hand or foot move onto a boulder problem. Remember you can go up, down, left or right, and if you forget the sequence you are out of the game. This is also a good exercise for improving your memory for a sequence.
- three ways – for any sequence or boulder problem, try to find at least three different ways of executing it. This is good for forcing you to try less attractive alternatives.
- deliberately seek out moves, rock types or holds you dislike. Keep the difficulty easy (perhaps top rope), but aim to get thoroughly immersed in, say, hand jamming, smearing, slate climbing or whatever it is you find unfamiliar. Approach it with curiosity – how can you best use these holds? What can you learn about this rock type?

- looking for rests – try to find 10 different resting positions on a route or problem somewhat below your limit. How many ways can you find a pause or opportunity to shake out?

Sometimes it pays to constrain our climbing in order to force ourselves to be creative and to learn how to use our body in different ways.[3] Climbing and clipping only with the right hand, or climbing only moving to holds that are behind us, only using dynamic movements, or just using smears for feet, are all practice constraints which can force us to problem solve. The greater the amount of variability in our practice, the bigger our repertoire of solutions becomes. Be sure to make your constraints practice specific to climbing and the movement challenges you want to be able to solve. For example, I'm not sure that climbing blindfolded necessarily helps develop creative movement, unless you intend to climb in the dark or where you cannot see your feet; so think about the application of your practice to real-life climbing situations. Udo Neuman has some great videos on YouTube on how to use a constraints-based approach to improve climbing movement creativity.

EFFECTIVE ROUTE PREVIEWING

Route previewing has been shown time and again to be linked to fewer mistakes on a route and more functional movement patterns (definite moves rather than exploratory moves).[4] I have noticed that indoors, climbers tend to do this more for harder routes, but don't bother much on their warm-up, and outdoors, less experienced climbers tend to route read less often, perhaps because the path of their climb is not clearly marked out in coloured holds! Regardless, route previewing is an important skill and one which bears practising, frequently, in order to build up a better memory for sequences. We know that more experienced climbers tend to 'chunk' the route into larger sections, and likely look at not just the movements but also rests and gear/clips. Undoubtedly, the more you climb, the easier it is to spot sequences or understand how to use particular holds, but think about actively seeking variety in your climbing practice – if you've spent years only climbing one rock type, then your ability to route read when you go on holiday elsewhere is going to be limited.

Whilst not linked to creativity per se, remember that one of the skills which tend to decline rapidly when a climber is anxious is their ability to scan the rock ahead and spot possibilities for movement.[5] Under stress, our eye gaze search area becomes smaller and closer in to the body, and that's when we can miss holds and our opportunities for creative movement decrease. Developing a deliberate scan strategy as mentioned previously can be a helpful tool for those moments when we are totally boxed and the stress levels are rising.

DECISION MAKING

The long winter indoor climbing on plastic can mean you miss out on decision making practice needed for outdoor routes, making these skills rusty. Particularly for onsight trad climbing, where we might need to make multiple decisions about route direction, foot- or hand-hold choice, nut/cam size choice, to extend or not to extend, and so on, plastic offers a very sanitised experience. If you are mainly indoor climbing, then making up your own routes or problems, or 'rainbowing' for feet or hands, can help you maintain that decision making capability. You could also think about taking some winter walks to new crags, and practise spotting lines, then checking back in the guidebook, or predicting what piece of gear might go where in a convenient crack. Think about all the decisions you might need to make on a route of your choice – how can you simulate and practise those decision making capabilities?

CONTINGENCY PLANNING

A skill not often practised by climbers, developing action plans for worst-case scenarios is something which can be liberating and allow for better decision making under stress. Many climbers avoid thinking about what might happen if they can't climb a crux section, if they get panicked on a route, fall off at an overhang and can't get back on, or if they run out of gear or if there is some other untoward event. Investing in some time with a qualified instructor can be helpful in drilling problem-solving, rope-work, etc., but spending some time thinking through the 'what-ifs' will have a beneficial impact psychologically. If situations can't be practised in a real-rock situation, then they can be practised using imagery, allowing rehearsal of the contingency plan with a successful outcome.

Exercise

Grab a piece of paper and spend some time thinking about the risks or potential problems which might occur at your chosen venue/ route/problem. Think about environmental factors, route/problem characteristics and your own strengths and weaknesses. When you have a decent list, figure out an action plan for what to do if each of these potential problems occurs. Note any equipment you need, and try to practise if possible. If you can't practise in real life, use the imagery instructions to help you go through the scenario in your imagination. This will work best if you have cues for the real thing around you – for example, having your harness and rack on, wearing your shoes and chalkbag, or being at the crag.

Climber study: Lara

Through some exploratory conversations, Lara realised that she had become too attached to getting each climb 'right'. She was very focused on precise movement and correct sequences. Whilst this meant she appeared to be a tidy, accurate and efficient climber, she was also stagnating a little and plateauing in her performance, particularly for onsight climbing.

We introduced the idea of improvisation in Lara's climbing, to help Lara to break out of her perfectionist way of climbing. Lara's top rope challenges were: (a) to climb routes that were too hard, and not to work the sequences, just to bypass any too-hard moves; (b) to figure out three different ways to climb a crux on the route and (c) to climb a route as fast as she could, not worrying about accuracy. She also played a game of trying to 'climb like Harry' – Harry was a climbing friend who was an entirely different size, shape and strength climber to Lara.

Whilst completing these challenges, Lara collected some data on how it felt to climb in these different ways. She realised that she had been climbing well below her ability by being overly focused on getting it just right, and that actually, she could get away with a lot more than she realised. This gave her the confidence to start trying harder routes, which she often sent by the skin of her teeth, helping her break out of her plateau.

SUMMARY

The key learning point from this chapter is to try to actively increase the variability of your climbing practice. Seek out new venues, new gyms, new route setters and new ways of climbing. Learning how to improvise and be creative in your movement patterns comes from actively giving yourself new challenges to solve, in an environment where it feels safe to do so. In this way, we have more tools in our toolbox to help us solve novel climbing problems when we encounter them for real, and our ability to take on bigger challenges is enhanced. Don't get too set in your ways – once you have any climbing anxieties under control, then start to seek out novelty to expand your comfort zone.

SECTION 3
Summary

The skills in section 3 have all been identified by research as important skilful climbing performance. They all take a lot of deliberate practice to learn well, but the good news is many can be practised when injured, during rest periods, warm-ups or simply when hanging out at the crag. Imagine for a moment if you spent the winter months focusing more on developing these mental skills than doing 4x4s or fingerboarding – you would have better concentration, movement efficiency and confidence, closing the gap between your potential and your actual climbing ability.

One of the reasons perhaps that people give up training the mental side is that it's hard to see tangible outcomes quickly, in the way that you do when you do strength or stamina training. But if you've been diligent about goal setting, you should be able to measure your progress just the same, and see the benefits in that inner confidence that comes from knowing your head is in a good place.

However, I think another reason people don't train their mental skills is perhaps because no one else seems to be doing it. If you don't see people at your local climbing gym with their notebooks and pens, practising focusing exercises or getting on very easy climbs to hone their problem-solving, then maybe you feel embarrassed to do so. I was coaching at a local wall recently and myself and the client were using a mindfulness exercise which involved mindful walking, pressing the feet into the floor. We probably did look a bit peculiar, but when I opened an eye to check on the client, the wall staff were laughing at us. It didn't bother me much, but it didn't help my client who was already feeling self-conscious due to anxiety.

So you are going to need to be a bit brave and face up to being perhaps the only one at the crag doing some mental preparation. That's ok
though right, we climbers don't mind being a bit different! And isn't it
worth it for the gains in your climbing performance?

CHAPTER **15**

Final thoughts

Climbing for life – mental wellbeing for climbers

We climbers are often known for being somewhat obsessional about our sport. There is nothing wrong with being passionate and throwing yourself wholeheartedly into climbing and improvement, but there are some downsides to watch out for. Some of the climbers I have worked with have, for one reason or another, been struggling with core beliefs which impact negatively on their climbing. For some, it's rigid and unhelpful perfectionism, where self-criticism really inhibits their performance and mental wellbeing. For others, it is struggles with their eating and diet, or for others, it is driving themselves too hard into overtraining and potential injury.

Maybe climbing as a sport attracts people who want to improve, to drive themselves forwards, and with its grading system it's easy to measure yourself against others as well as your own past performance. There is also an immersive culture which emphasises improvement, training, being stronger and trying harder. As a climber, if you take a dip into social media, you are instantly surrounded by fit, toned, ripped bodies, pulling hard. Maybe this is inspiring to you, but maybe these elements also cause some negative self-comparisons and doubts? The gap now between elite climbers and 'weekend warriors' is huge and growing. Many ordinary climbers will struggle to see 'someone like me' on Instagram, in training videos and so on, and that can result in dissatisfaction and deepening worries, concerns or insecurities. We are just starting to realise the numbers of climbers struggling with their mental health, and to think about how our sport can both lift people's mental wellbeing and also contribute to those difficulties. How should we foster a healthy attitude towards improvement, without falling into any of the traps that lie in wait for us?

PERFECTIONISM

One of the key traits that cause trouble for some climbers is perfectionism. Perfectionism, where we have very high standards for ourselves (and sometimes others), is not necessarily a bad thing in and of itself, and on the one hand, it can push us to improve. However, unhealthy perfectionism, where adherence to those very high standards is unrelenting, rigid and absolute, can be very problematic, and is often at the root of some of the other issues climbers may face with eating, overtraining, poor performance under pressure and mental health problems.

How do you know you have unhealthy perfectionism? There are lots of online quizzes you can take with varying levels of validity,[1] but the bottom line is this: if your high standards are making you miserable and you feel like you are constantly disappointing yourself and others, or others constantly disappoint you, then your perfectionism isn't working for you. If you cannot come to terms with mistakes, faux pas, average results or off days fairly quickly (within a day or two) and find yourself ruminating endlessly over what you did wrong, and it doesn't motivate you to find ways to do better next time, then perfectionism is not working for you. If you are rarely satisfied with your performance and have a loud and insistent inner critic who is rarely quiet, and are constantly negatively comparing yourself with others, then it's likely that you have an unhealthy perfectionism. The impact of this long term can be to sap your enjoyment of the sport, decrease motivation, develop a 'play it safe' attitude and, at its extremes, develop low mood, depression and self-harmful behaviours.

In an ideal world, we would be able to harness the helpful aspects of perfectionism, turning it on and off like a tap when we most need it. Perfectionism can be helpful in terms of following a training program for example, or when you need to prep for something really important, but when it comes to the crunch, we need to be able to turn the tap off and let our prep speak for itself. It's also unhelpful to have the tap on when we are analysing our performance afterwards, since here we need to have a curious and open mindset, rather than an absolutist one. Recognising when perfectionism is at play is the first step to being able to turn the tap off and on at will.

Sometimes there is a fear that if we let go of our perfectionism, then we will be lazy, a total failure or even disliked and unloved. It is worth thinking about where these beliefs might have come from, in order to understand the role perfectionism is playing in your life. Often these traits have been with us for a long time; perhaps the main message of our childhood was that we were only noticed for our achievements, or heavily criticised for any mistakes. Sometimes, our own high motivation for the sport from a young age can drive us to train hard before we are emotionally ready, or sometimes a coach can believe they are driving us to excel, but in reality they are reinforcing perfectionism.

Sometimes our inner critic is an echo of past criticisms we have received. Our early experiences are powerful in shaping our inner self-talk, but as we mature, we start to experience that inner voice as our own, and it becomes harder therefore to discount it. However, no matter how believable it is in that moment, it is still only a thought, a product of our brain cells firing. You might also remember that this same brain is capable of producing thoughts about what you want for dinner, the name of the lead singer of Wham, how bats pooh upside down, why it's a good idea to mix sambuca and beer, and other random thoughts at inopportune moments of the day! And it can also produce thoughts which are confident and positive about our abilities. The point is, it does not always pay to listen to and believe your thoughts and inner voices, particularly when you are halfway up a cliff face.

Exercise: Understanding thought and meaning associations[2]

Do you remember the 'milk' exercise from chapter 5? Try saying the word 'milk' out loud again. Notice what happens – do you get an image in your mind of a glass of milk? A carton of oat milk? Do you think about the taste or having it in your tea? Do you think about making pancakes with milk, or do you see images of cows in fields? Are you now craving a cup of coffee, or thinking about that latte you had with your friend? Notice how many associated thoughts you get as you think about milk and where your mind takes you. Now try saying the word 'milk' over and over again. What happens now? Try it faster and faster or in a funny voice. What happens now? What happens to those associated thoughts and images? Do they begin to dissolve into just a noise?

This exercise is helpful for understanding that no matter how powerful our thoughts are, they are in fact just made up of words, letters and noises, derived from electrical impulses in our brain. We don't have to pay attention to them, even if they do seem very real to us. You can try this exercise with any 'loaded' words you regularly use in self-criticism.

WHAT CAN I DO ABOUT PERFECTIONISM?

First, it's important to notice when you are engaging in perfectionist thinking. Typically, this is where you think in very absolutist or all-or-nothing terms, for example, 'If I don't send this route, I may as well give up climbing'; 'I must never mess up a sequence'. Noticing when you tend to think like this, and which situations might trigger perfectionist thinking, can be a helpful first step. Using a thought record can be useful to capture some examples for you to work with.

You can also try to dig down a little into the beliefs that might underlie these thoughts. The downward arrow technique is a helpful way to uncover what core beliefs might lie at the heart of the perfectionist thinking you lean towards.

When you notice yourself thinking in very absolutist and negative terms, you have two options: either to challenge your unhelpful beliefs, or to unhook from them. Challenging your beliefs follows the same principles we used previously – how true is this (0–100%), how likely is this to happen (0–100%), what might someone else think about this, is there another way to look at this? You can also use the two exercises below to challenge or unhook.

Exercise: Challenging your core beliefs

At the heart of perfectionism thinking can be some pretty harsh if-then beliefs. 'If I'm not perfect, then I'm useless', 'If I don't get it just right, then I'm hopeless', 'If I don't win, then I'm a failure' and 'if I make a mistake, then my partner will leave me' are common examples of if-then-type beliefs. We can uncover these using the downward arrow technique. When you get to the bottom and find your core belief or core fear, think about how much you believe this on a scale of 0–100% and write this down.

Now turn over the paper, and think about the opposite of this core belief or core fear. For example, the opposite of useless might be useful, the opposite of being a failure might be a success, and so on. When you have the opposite, try to define what it means. What 5–10 key characteristics make up this quality? So if you are thinking about success, then what does successful mean? What key characteristics make someone a success? List them out individually. There is an example below to help you using the belief of being a successful climber, from the opposite belief of being a failure as a climber. Then I want you to score yourself on each characteristic (but not the main concept) from 0 to 100%. Now think about the main concept – to what extent do you now believe you embody this? Remember, you are not trying to convince yourself that you are not a failure or whatever it is; you are just trying to introduce cognitive doubt to this fixed belief.

Example: How to be a successful climber

Characteristic	*Belief 0–100%*
Train hard	*90%*
Be strategic on routes	*55%*
Good analytical skills to work on weaknesses	*75%*
Clear goals	*30%*
Seek help and advice from others	*45%*
Good technique	*60%*

To what extent do I now think I am a successful climber 60%

This exercise also helps you to understand how you can move towards embodying this important characteristic. In the example above, it's easy to spot that working on clarifying goals and being more strategic on routes will enhance the sense of success.

Exercise: Unhooking from perfectionist thoughts

Imagine you are sitting next to a stream, watching the water run by. Every now and then, a leaf drops into the stream, and you can watch it float down the river until it is out of sight. Try to keep watching the leaves on the stream in your mind's eye. As your thoughts arise, imagine placing each one onto a leaf, and watching it drift downstream. You can imagine your perfectionist thoughts and self-criticisms as written on leaves drifting down the stream. Any time you notice these thoughts arising, imagine them floating by as you watch them, separate to you, coming and going.

These techniques are very similar to those we used to deal with any anxious thoughts in trying to introduce doubt to the underlying belief, and unhooking from those thoughts when they arise, so we can see ourselves as separate to our thoughts.

Climber study – Janey

Janey was part of a competition squad and found herself struggling with a lot of negative and highly critical thoughts in the run-up to competitions and afterwards when she didn't perform so well. It was hard for her initially to describe the content of the thoughts, so we spent a couple of weeks using the thought record form to capture the content. Janey realised her negative thoughts were a kind of automatic habit and happened at many points during the day, including outside of climbing. It seemed as though her mind was trying to protect her from failure, and so she was preparing herself in a pessimistic way for possible negative outcomes. Once she recognised that this was an attempt by her mind to be helpful, she was able to use some unhooking techniques (breathing out the thoughts and breathing in what she had gained from her training) before competitions.

However, the self-flagellation after the comps was harder to undo. Janey's parents videoed as much of the comps as they could, and Janey was prone to pore over these videos and pick out every wrong move or decision. This led to a rumination cycle where she tipped into further self-criticism, leading to thoughts like 'I'll never be any good' and 'the team is going to drop me pretty soon'. Janey was left feeling pretty depressed about her climbing in the week or so after the comp.

To tackle this, first we mapped out the downward spiral of her thoughts. Janey was able to see that with an eye only for what she did wrong, she was leading herself into a negative rumination cycle. By changing the focus to what she did right in the comps, she was able to weaken the rumination cycle. Next we used the downward arrow technique to look at what was so bad about getting dropped from the team. Janey was able to identify that her beliefs were about how shameful and embarrassing it would be to be dropped from the team. Challenging this thought was hard, as climbing was so important to Janey, but she was able to see that she could still climb even if not part of the team, and that she wouldn't want to be on the team if she wasn't up to it anyway – the team were supposed to be good climbers. This led Janey to realise that as she was still on the team, then she must be good enough to be there. Due to the shame associated with her thoughts about being 'found out' as not good enough for the team, I encouraged her to share the thoughts with her coach and parents, to take away the secrecy. They were able to reassure her that she belonged there, but even if she didn't perform well at comps, she still had lots of potential as a climber. We spent some time mapping out what makes a climber with potential, and Janey was able to see that she already had some of these characteristics, and the rest she could work on.

HEALTHY ATTITUDES TOWARDS DIET AND EATING

It is only in the last year or so that elite climbers have begun to talk openly about their struggles with disordered eating and RED-S (where climbers chronically underfuel, which can be linked to difficulties with body image),[3] and it is fantastic that they now feel safe to do so. The incidence of eating disorders such as anorexia, bulimia and RED-S in sport climbing is estimated to be higher than the general population,[4] and even this is likely to be an underestimate because we simply don't have enough accurate data. What is it then about climbing which creates the conditions to foster difficulties with eating, and how can we protect young climbers against that?

Climbing has long been thought of as a lean sport, and the idea persists that losing weight is a good way to maximise the strength you have, despite the dangers associated with restricted diets. Anorexia has the highest mortality rate of any mental health problem,[5] and prolonged underfuelling can lead to hormonal dysfunction, cardiovascular problems, immune deficiency and poorer bone health.[6] When our body mass index falls below a certain level, our brain functions change and our thinking becomes more rigid and fixed, making it harder to escape the tyranny of eating difficulties.[7] We know that perfectionism can be linked to problems with eating, and eating difficulties can also sometimes be driven by needing a sense of control, especially under high stress.

However, the images and narratives within climbing culture may play a role too. A study found that young female athletes were particularly susceptible to negative body image, when they were shown images of very thin, older female athletes in revealing outfits.[8] When we think of the images in popular media, there are an abundance of images of men and women which emphasise lean, muscular bodies. Our sport looks like a body-conscious sport, and the implicit message is you need to look like this to be a climber. Couple this with the endless discussions on forums and social media about 'nutrition' which is more often about the best diet in the restrictive sense of the word – paleo, vegan, etc. – and rarely written by a registered dietician. If this strikes a chord for you, I would consider whether it might be prudent to stop consuming climbing media, and detach from the imagery which might be feeding a negative cycle of self-evaluation.

Coaches and anyone in a position of being a role model (including elite athletes) need to be mindful of what they show to those who look up to them. They will, whether they like it or not, be scrutinised for what they eat, how they talk about their bodies and food, and the images they release. Unfortunately, it is not possible to avoid being a role model if you are in the limelight or a position of influence in our small community, and acknowledging this is an important first step in understanding the impact of what you say and do on other climbers. Think about how you talk about food, eating, weight and body image; what are you modelling to other climbers?

HOW DO I KNOW IF I HAVE UNHEALTHY ATTITUDES TOWARDS FOOD AND EATING?

Eating disorders tend to be insidious in onset, and it can be hard to pinpoint when they start. Feeling very down about your body, very self-critical about your weight, and seeing food as punishment or reward can be some early indicators that you may have some difficulties with food and body image. Likewise, if you tend to feel anxious about having to eat in front of others, about celebration meals such as Christmas, or are very restrictive about what food groups and types you can and can't eat, then these are indicators that your attitudes towards food are less healthy.

Whilst disordered eating is often thought of as affecting predominantly women, men are also affected and the stigma may be even greater for them, when resources are typically aimed at women and girls. There are many expressions of unhealthy attitudes towards food and eating; orthorexia (an obsession with eating healthily), anorexia (severe restriction in calorie intake), bulimia (where there may be a cycle of binge eating and followed by purging by vomiting or use of laxatives), and sometimes RED-S can develop due to underlying concerns about weight and body image.

HOW CAN I OVERCOME MY DIFFICULTIES WITH EATING?

Due to the risks involved, this is not something you want to try to tackle alone, but the first step is acknowledging that you need help. It is very important that you seek help, through working with a registered dietician and a registered psychologist. Your GP will be able to refer you to your local Eating Disorders team. This can be a scary step and you may feel frightened of gaining weight, but the aim will be to get you to a healthy weight and help you tackle the underlying issues so food becomes just fuel again.

If you are a friend or family member, or a coach, then the person you are worried about may not be ready to ask for help, but you can still offer. The best thing you can do is to tell them you are worried about **them**, not their weight. Try not to talk about their weight loss, but focus on connecting with them as a person and offer to listen. Coaches need to be mindful of not commenting on weight loss or gain and linking weight with performance. There are some great self-help resources out there, which can be a helpful adjunct to treatment and so coaches, family and friends can support the climber they are worried about. Check out the BEAT website[9] for a good starting point.

MENTAL HEALTH AND CLIMBING

Whilst being in nature certainly has positive influences on our mental health, and exercise is good for us, is there something special about climbing which could enhance our wellbeing? And conversely, might there be something about climbing which could negatively impact our wellbeing?

There is something beguiling about climbing when it is going well – total absorption in a mindful sport, well supported by a close-knit community, with opportunities to challenge ourselves in beautiful environments. When we have a good day, a good week or a good run, we can feel strong, brave, exhilarated and part of something bigger than ourselves.

But what about when it's not going well? What about when we feel we don't fit in, we are making no progress, and negative experiences start to outweigh the positive? Or when what is happening in our wider life starts to leak into our climbing? Could there be something about climbers' personalities perhaps which might make them more vulnerable to anxiety or other mental health difficulties?

Risk factors for mental health problems include environmental factors like poverty, stigma and discrimination and being subject to trauma – external factors which undermine our sense of agency and power and reduce our opportunities. Social isolation is also a huge factor in mental health difficulties; we are social animals and meaningful connections with others are central to our mental wellbeing. There are also internal processes which can lead to mental health difficulties, such as rigid and inflexible thought patterns and beliefs, and fusing with our thoughts and feelings, as though we are only the contents our thoughts and feelings.

We can enhance our mental wellbeing and become more resilient to life's curve balls. We can do this by cultivating optimism, connecting with our values and having a sense of purpose in our lives, adopting healthy habits (of mind and body – sleep, nutrition and healthy thinking patterns), learning to manage our emotions, connecting to others and embracing the learning wherever it shows up in our lives. We call this *psychological flexibility*,[10] and it is something which can be learnt rather than being something you have or not. There is an exercise for developing optimism at the end of this chapter, but many of the exercises in this book provide ways of helping you to become more psychologically flexible, and can benefit your wellbeing.

Fluctuations in our mood and wellbeing are normal, but if you find yourself feeling low or anxious for more than a few weeks, then think about what is going on for you. If you do find that your mental health difficulties are impacting on your sleep and appetite, work, friendships, intimate relationships and sense of drive, then please do talk to someone you can trust as a first step. You are not alone, and there are more options now than there ever were in terms of accessing professional help. Talk to your GP, look up the resources available from MIND[11] or look for a qualified therapist via the BABCP database if you are in the UK. If you find yourself having thoughts of suicide, or making plans or preparations, then you can call the Samaritans at any time of day or night on 116 123. Don't try to manage alone.

STAYING PSYCHED: MOTIVATION

It's normal and natural for our motivation to climb to come and go in waves, so try not to get too worried if you don't feel much like climbing or training for a few weeks. You'll remember at the beginning of this book, I suggested building in some downtime to conserve your motivation for training. It's not realistic to be psyched the whole time, especially if your routine stays the same. Being intrinsically motivated is linked with longer-term participation in sports, and intrinsic motivation is linked to autonomy, competence and good relationships.[12]

If your motivation is flagging, consider whether one of these three pillars might be missing for you. Have you neglected to develop your technique, or have you been training so hard you are not getting some quick successes in to keep you feeling good? Has the challenge level been so high that you just feel rubbish about your abilities? Do you feel as though you have a sense of control over your climbing, or is anxiety or even a coach running the show without your input? Most importantly, does your climbing give you a sense of connection with other people, or are you feeling alienated and disconnected for some reason? And what did you first love about climbing when you started – what got you hooked? Are your current climbing practices in sync with what first grabbed you all those years ago, or have you drifted away from your values?

It can also be hard when a sport which has formed such a big part of our lives no longer gives us the same joy and rewards. However, you cannot force motivation; all you can do is provide the right conditions for it to occur. Recognising when to take a break, when to change tack, when to mix things up and when to quit (your climbing gym, climbing partner or even climbing itself) is an important skill to learn also. Climbing will always be there for you, so if motivation is low, then consider whether your current climbing practices have you a little burnt out, take a break and reflect on what happened. Climbing has one of the largest participation age ranges of any sport,[13] so there is good evidence to suggest that once hooked, climbing grabs us for life, even if what motivates us changes as we age. If you love climbing, that love will return, and one look around the crags and gyms will tell you that there is no upper age limit for our sport, so you have plenty of time to rest and recharge.

BALANCE

Such a simple word, yet striving for balance in all things can be extremely difficult, particularly in an immersive sport like climbing, where no one says, 'I climb', they tend to say, 'I'm a climber'. The sport tends to stand for our whole personal identity, and any perceived failure in our climbing can have a profound impact on how we feel about ourselves.

Whilst being so immersed in a sport might seem like a good thing, it's interesting to look at other successful sports cultures to see how they manage personhood whilst being a sports person. For example, the New Zealand Rugby Team, the All Blacks, one of the most successful rugby teams of all time, have a motto, 'better people make better All Blacks',[14] a motto which emphasises the need for developing your whole character, not just sport-relevant attributes. Elite athletes nowadays are encouraged to keep other aspects of their life going – family, friends, career or education – to give them perspective outside their sport and to balance out the continuously high demands. I think this is a helpful idea to consider – how can you make sure that you look after the whole of your personhood, not just the climber in you? Think back to the exercises right at the beginning of this book, where you mapped out your life values and climbing values. What actions are you taking to bring your values to life each day, each week? Do your climbing values have a sense of balance, and include more than just training and climbing hard? Are you still connecting with what you love about the sport?

At a broader level, we know from the positive psychology literature that having meaningful connections with others, having a sense of purpose in your life and being optimistic will have a good impact on your resilience and mental health. Optimism is actually something which can be developed believe it or not, so if you are someone who tends to see the glass as half empty, then there is an exercise below to help you shift that pessimistic mindset. You can also challenge your pessimistic beliefs using the core beliefs exercise from the perfectionism section.

Exercise: Gratitude journal

Spend a couple of minutes at the end of each day, just before you go to sleep, noting down two or three things you are grateful for. They don't have to be big things, small occurrences like having someone make you a cup of tea at work, for the friend that sent you a funny GIF or coming in to a quiet house at the end of a busy day. Just note down anything that you are thankful for. Research has shown that gratitude journaling can have a positive impact on your wellbeing and sense of optimism.[15]

At the end of the day, all the exercises in this book, all the mental training techniques, are nothing if you don't enjoy your sport and have fun. For me, the main reason to improve your headgame is to enjoy climbing more, and be able to challenge yourself in enjoyable ways. The training may take hard work and dedication, but if there is no fun in it, and you are forcing yourself to do it, then your motivation is likely to suffer. The British climber Shauna Coxsey is well known for goofing around with her climbing coach and friend Leah Crane, and at her talk for the Women's Climbing Symposium in 2021, she spoke about the need for training and climbing to be fun for her, and if it wasn't fun, she just couldn't do it. I think it is possible to be both dedicated and to hold our sport lightly, as just one piece of the beautiful and unique jigsaw that makes up who we are.

Notes

CHAPTER 1

1 (Horst, 2008)
2 (Jones & Sanchez, 2017)
3 (Sanchez, Torregrossa, Woodman, Jones, & Llewellyn, 2019)
4 (Kingston & Wilson, 2008)
5 (Sanchez, Torregrossa, Woodman, Jones, & Llewellyn, 2019)
6 (Dupuy & Ripoll, 1989)
7 (Jones & Sanchez, 2017)
8 (Seifert, Orth, Button, & Davids, 2017)
9 (Orth, Button, Davids, & Seifert, 2017)
10 (Seifert, Orth, Button, & Davids, 2017)
11 (Bandura, 1977)
12 (Sanchez & Torregrossa, 2005)
13 (Jones & Sanchez, 2017)
14 (Gill, Williams, & Refisteck, 2017)
15 (Pjipers, Oudejans, Bakker, & Beek, 2006)
16 (Perry, 2020)
17 https://smartclimbing.co.uk/product/climbing-skills-assessment-pdf/
18 (Horst, 2008)

CHAPTER 2

1 (Doran, 1981)
2 (Dixon, 2008)
3 (Prochaska & DiClemente, 1983)
4 Adapted from Harris (2019)
5 (Harris, 2007)
6 (Perry, 2020)
7 (Hawkins, Crust, Swann, & Jackman, 2020)

CHAPTER 3

1 (Vanderkam, 2018)
2 (Lally, van Jaarsveld, Potts, & Wardle, 2010)
3 (Clear, 2018)
4 See Self Determination Theory (Deci & Ryan, 1985)
5 (Gordon, Chester, & Denton, 2015)

CHAPTER 4

1 (Gilbert, 2015) (Blakey & Abramowitz, 2016)
2 (Haines, 2018)
3 (Peters, 2012)
4 (Purdon, 2004)
5 (Zerubavel & Messman-Moore, 2013)
6 (Harris, 2015)
7 (Salkovskis, 1991)

CHAPTER 5

1 (Cloninger, Cloninger, Zwir, & Keltikangas-Jarvinen, 2019)
2 Yerkes-Dodson Curve, adapted from Slavin (2018)
3 (Zaccaro et al., 2018)
4 (Zaccaro et al., 2018)
5 (Beck & Beck, 2011)
6 (Harris, 2019)
7 (Kabat Zinn, 2016)
8 (Hegarty & Huelsmann, 2020)
9 Adapted from Harris (2007)
10 (Singh, Singh, Adkins, Singh, & Winton, 2008)
11 (Wolpe, 1990; McKay, Abramowitz, & Storch, 2019)
12 (Wenzlaff & Wegner, 2000; Abramowitz, Tolin, & Street, 2001)
13 (Iijima & Tanno, 2012)

CHAPTER 6

1 Exercises adapted from the *Smart Climbing Fear of Falling Workbook* (Williams, 2021)
2 (Pageaux & Lepers, 2018)
3 (Raue, Streicher, Lermer, & Frey, 2019)

CHAPTER 7

1 (Kirsch, Lynn, Vigorito, & Miller, 2004)
2 (Nutt & Sharpe, 2008)
3 (Maier & Seligman, 1976)
4 (Woodman, Hardy, Barlow, & Le Scanff, 2010)

CHAPTER 8

1 (Raue, Streicher, Lermer & Frey, 2019)
2 (Hardy & Parfitt, 1991)

CHAPTER 9

1 (Draper et al., 2011)
2 (Barradas & Lencastre, 2021)

CHAPTER 10

1 (Keegan, Harwood, Spray, & Lavallee, 2011)
2 (Keegan, Harwood, Spray, & Lavallee, 2011)
3 (Dweck, 2006)
4 (Strosahl, Wilson, & Hayes, 1999)

CHAPTER 11

1   (Bandura, 1977)

2   (Hayes, Laurenceau, Feldman, Strauss & Cardaciotta, 2007; Vealey & Chase, 2008; Bandura, 1977)

3   (Rubin, 1986)

4   (Luft & Ingham, 1961)

5   (Berry, 2018)

6   (Hardy & Oliver, 2014)

7   (Gonzalez-Rosa et al., 2015)

8   (Deci & Ryan, 1985)

CHAPTER 12

1   (Baddeley, 2011)

2   (Lyddy & Good, 2017)

3   (Bell & Hardy, 2009)

4   (Sanchez, Torregrossa, Woodman, Jones, & Llewellyn, 2019)

5   (Maynard & Crisfield, 1998)

6   (Sanchez, Torregrossa, Woodman, Jones, & Llewellyn, 2019)

7   (Csikszentmihalyi, 2008; Jackson & Csikszentmihalyi, 1999)

8   (Csikszentmihalyi, 2008)

9   (Hardy & Parfitt, 1991)

10 (Jackson & Csikszentmihalyi, 1999)

11 (Clarke, Sheffield, & Akehurst, 2020)

CHAPTER 13

1   (Decety, 1996)

2   (Zeman, Dewar & Della Sala, 2015)

3   (Holmes & Collins, 2001)

4   See Reel Rock 13 (Barr & Lowell, 2018)

5   (Smith, Wright, Allsopp & Westhead, 2007)

6 (Arvinen-Barrow, Clement & Hemmings, 2013)

7 (Melzack, 2011)

8 (Pincus & Sheikh, 2009)

9 (Pain Management. Meditation for pain relief, n.d.)

CHAPTER 14

1 (Orth, van der Kamp, Memmert & Savelsbergh, 2017)

2 (Smith, 2009)

3 (Orth, Davids & Seifert, 2016)

4 (Seifert, Cordier, Orth, Courtine & Croft, 2017)

5 (Button, Orth, Davids & Seifert, 2017)

CHAPTER 15

1 See Psychology Today (https://www.psychologytoday.com/gb/tests/personality/perfectionism-test)

2 (Masuda, Hayes, Sackett & Twohig, 2004)

3 See https://www.ukclimbing.com/articles/features/relative_energy_deficiency_in_sport_-_a_cautionary_tale-12345 (Leslie-Wujastyk, 2019)

4 (Gibson-Smith, Storey & Ranchordas, 2020)

5 (Chesney, Goodwin, & Fazel, 2014)

6 (Meczekalski, Podfigurna-Stopa & Katulski, 2013)

7 (Steegers et al., 2021)

8 (Teixidor-Batlle, Ventura & Andres, 2021)

9 See https://www.beateatingdisorders.org.uk/

10 See also Hexaflex model (Hayes, Strosahl & Wilson, 2011)

11 See MIND website https://www.mind.org.uk/

12 (Deci & Ryan, 1985)

13 (Gordon, Chester & Denton, 2015)

14 (Hodge, Henry & Smith, 2014)

15 (Cheng, Tsui & Lam, 2015)

References

Abramowitz, J., Tolin, D. F., & Street, G. P. (2001). Paradoxical effects of thought suppression: A meta-analysis of controlled studies. *Clinical Psychology Review, 21*(5), 683–703.

Arvinen-Barrow, M., Clement, D., & Hemmings, B. (2013). Imagery in sport injury rehabilitation. In M. Arvinen-Barrow, & N. Walker, *The Psychology of Sport Injury and Rehabilitation* (p. 15). London: Routledge.

Baddeley, A. (2011). Working memory: Theories, models, and controversies. *Annual Review of Psychology, 63*, 1–29.

Bandura, A. (1977). Self-efficacy: Towards a unifying theory of behavioral change. *Psychological Review, 84*(2), 191–215.

Barr, Z., Lowell, J. (Producers), Lowell, J., Barr, Z., & Mortimer, P. (Directors). (2018). *Reel Rock 13* [Motion Picture].

Barradas, R., & Lencastre, J. A. (2021). Gamification and game-based learning: Strategies to promote positive competitiveness in the teaching and learning processes. In J. A. Lencastre, P. Spanu, G. Ilin, P. Milios, & M. Bento, *Gaming in Action* (pp. 51–75). Istanbul: Mesleki Girisimciler ve Toplum Gonulluleri Dernegi.

Beck, J. S., & Beck, A. T. (2011). *Cognitive Behavior Therapy: Basics and Beyond* (2nd ed.). New York: Guildford Press.

Bell, J. J., & Hardy, J. (2009). Effects of attentional focus on skilled performance in Golf. *Journal of Applied Sport Psychology, 21*, 163–177.

Berry, N. (2018, July 6). *Indian Face E9 6c by Angus Killie*. Retrieved from ukclimbing.com: https://www.ukclimbing.com/news/2018/07/indian_face_e9_6c_by_angus_kille-71634

Boulougouris, J. C., & Marks, I. M. (1969). Implosion (flooding)-a new treatment for phobias. *British Medical Journal, 2*, 721–723.

Button, C., Orth, D., Davids, K., & Seifert, L. (2017). Visual-motor skill in climbing. In L. Seifert, P. Wolf, & A. Schweizer, *The Science of Climbing and Mountaineering* (pp. 210–224). London: Routledge.

Cheng, S.-T., Tsui, P. K., & Lam, J. H. (2015). Improving mental health in healthcare practitioners: Randomized control trial of a gratitude intervention. *Journal of consulting and clinical psychology, 83*(1), 177.

Chesney, E., Goodwin, G. M., & Fazel, S. (2014). Risks of all-cause and suicide mortality in mental disorders: a meta-review. *World Psychiatry, 13*(2), 153–160.

Clarke, P., Sheffield, D., & Akehurst, S. (2020). Personality predictors of yips and choking susceptibility. *Frontiers in Psychology, 10*. Article 2784, 1–15

Clear, J. (2018). *Atomic Habits: An Easy & Proven Way to Build Good Habits & Break Bad Ones*. New York: Random House.

Cloninger, C. R., Cloninger, K. M., Zwir, I., & Keltikangas-Jarvinen, L. (2019). The complex genetics and biology of human temperament: A review of traditional concepts in relation to new molecular findings. *Translational Psychiatry, 9*, 290.

Covey, S. (1994). *Daily Reflections for Highly Effective People: Living the 7 Habits of Highly Effective People Every Day*. New York: Touchstone.

Csikszentmihalyi, M. (2008). *Flow: The Psychology of Optimal Experience*. New York: Harper Perennial.

Decety, J. (1996). The neurophysiological basis of motor imagery. *Behavioural Brain Research, 77*(1), 45–52.

Deci, E. L., & Ryan, R. M. (1985). *Intrinsic Motivation and Self-Determination in Human Behavior*. New York: Plenum.

Dixon, A. (2008). *Motivation and Confidence: What Does It Take to Change behaviour?* London: The Kings Fund.

Doran, G. (1981). There's a S.M.A.R.T. way to write management's goals and objectives. *Management Review, 70*, 35–36.

Draper, N., Dickson, T., Blackwell, G., Fryer, S., Priestley, S., Winter, D., & Ellis, G. (2011). Self-reported ability assessment in rock climbing. *Journal of Sports Sciences, 29*, 851–858.

Dupuy, C., & Ripoll, H. (1989). Analyse des stratégies visuo-motrices en escalade sportive. *Revue Siences et Motricité, 7*, 19–26.

Dweck, C. S. (2006). *Mindset: The New Psychology of Success*. New York: Random House.

Gibson-Smith, E., Storey, R., & Ranchordas, M. (2020). Dietary intake, body composition and iron status in experienced and elite climbers. *Frontiers in Nutrition, 7*, 122.

Gilbert, P. (2015). An evolutionary approach to emotion in mental health with a focus on affiliative emotions. *Emotion Review, 7*, 1–8.

Gill, D. L., Williams, L., & Reifsteck, E. J. (2017). *Psychological Dynamics of Sport and Exercise* (4th ed.). Leeds: Human Kinetics.

Gonzalez-Rosa, J. J., Natali, F., Tettamanti, A., Cursi, M., Velikova, S., Comi, G., . . . Leocani, L. (2015). Action observation and motor imagery in performance of complex movements: Evidence from EEG and kinematics analysis. *Behavioural Brain Research, 281*, 290–300.

Gordon, K., Chester, M., & Denton, A. (2015). *Getting Active Outdoors*. Outdoor Industries Association; Sport England. Retrieved from https://www.sportengland.org/media/3275/outdoors-participation-report-v2-lr-spreads.pdf

Haines, S. (2018). *Anxiety is Really Strange*. London: Jessica Kingsley Publishers, Ltd.

Hardy, J., & Oliver, E. J. (2014). Self-talk, positive thinking and thought stopping. In R. C. Eklund, & G. Tenenbaum, *Encyclopedia of Sport and Exercise Psychology*. Thousand Oaks: SAGE.

Hardy, L., & Parfitt, G. (1991). A catastrophe model of anxiety and performance. *The British Psychological Society, 82*(2), 163–178.

Harris, R. (2007). *The Happiness Trap: Stop Struggling, Start Living*. Boston: Little, Brown Book Group.

Harris, R. (2015, Nov 2). The Struggle Switch [Video]. YouTube. Retrieved from https://www.youtube.com/watch?v=rCp1I16GCXI

Harris, R. (2019). *ACT Made Simple* (2nd ed.). Oakland, California: New Harbinger Publications, Inc.

Hawkins, R. M., Crust, L., Swann, C., & Jackman, P. C. (2020). The effects of goal types on psychological outcomes in active and insufficiently active adults in a walking task: Further evidence for open goals. *Psychology of Sport and Exercise, 48*, 101661

Hayes, A. M., Laurenceau, J.-P., Feldman, G., Strauss, J. L., & Cardaciotta, L. (2007). Change is not always linear: The study of nonlinear and discontinuous patterns of change in psychotherapy. *Clinical Psychological Review, 27*(6), 715–723.

Hayes, S. C., Strosahl, K. D., & Wilson, K. G. (2011). *Acceptance and Commitment Therapy: The Process and Practice of Mindful Change.* New York: Guilford Press.

Hegarty, J., & Huelsmann, C. (2020). *ACT IN SPORT: Improve Performance through Mindfulness, Acceptance, and Commitment.* Oakamoor: Dark River.

Hodge, K., Henry, G., & Smith, W. (2014). A case study of excellence in elite sport: Motivational climate in a world champion team. *The Psychologist, 28*, 60–74.

Holmes, P. S., & Collins, D. J. (2001). The PETTLEP approach to motor imagery: A functional equivalence model for sport psychologists. *Journal of Applied Sport Psychology, 13*(1), 60–83.

Horst, E. (2008). *Training for Climbing* (2nd ed.). Helena: Falcon Guides.

Iijima, Y., & Tanno, Y. (2012). The rebound effect in the unsuccessful suppression of worrisome thoughts. *Personality and Individual Differences, 53*(3), 347–350.

Jackson, S. A., & Csikszentmihalyi, M. (1999). *Flow in Sports.* Champaign: Human Kinetics.

Jones, G., & Sanchez, X. (2017). Psychological processes in the sport of climbing. In L. Seifert, P. Wolf, & A. Schweizer, *The Science of Climbing and Mountaineering* (pp. 243–256). Abingdon: Routledge.

Kabat Zinn, J. (2016). *Wherever You Go, There You Are.* Boston: Little, Brown Book Club.

Keegan, R., Harwood, C., Spray, C., & Lavallee, D. (2011). From 'motivational climate' to 'motivational atmosphere': A review of research examining the social and environmental influences on athlete motivation in sport. In B. D. Geranto, *Sport Psychology* (pp. 1–69). Hauppauge: Nova Science Publishers.

Kingston, K., & Wilson, K. (2008). The application of goal setting in sport. In *Advances in Applied Sport Psychology* (pp. 85–133). London: Routledge

Kirsch, I., Lynn, S. J., Vigorito, M., & Miller, R. R. (2004). The role of cognition in classical and operant conditioning. *Journal of Clinical Psychology, 60*(4), 369–392.

Lally, P., van Jaarsveld, C. H., Potts, H. W., & Wardle, J. (2010). How are habits formed: Modelling habit formation in the real world. *European Journal of Social Psychology, 40*, 998–1009. doi:10.1002/ejsp.674

Leslie-Wujastyk, M. (2019, October 21). *Relative Energy Deficiency in Sport - A Cautionary Tale.* Retrieved from ukclimbing.com: https://www.ukclimbing.com/articles/features/relative_energy_deficiency_in_sport_-_a_cautionary_tale-12345

Luft, J., & Ingham, H. (1961). The Johari Window: A graphic model of awareness in interpersonal relations. *Human Relations Training News, 5*(9), 6–7.

Lyddy, C. J., & Good, D. J. (2017). Being while doing: An inductive model of mindfulness at work. *Frontiers in Psychology, 7*, 2060.

Maier, S. F., & Seligman, M. E. (1976). Learned helplessness: Theory and evidence. *Journal of Experimental Psychology, 105*(1), 3–46.

Masuda, A., Hayes, S. C., Sackett, C. F., & Twohig, M. P. (2004). Cognitive defusion and self-relevant negative thoughts: Examining the impact of a ninety year old technique. *Behaviour Research and Therapy*, 477–485.

Maynard, I., & Crisfield, P. (1998). *Improving Concentration.* Leeds: Coachwise 1st4sport.

McKay, D., Abramowitz, J., & Storch, E. (2019). Ineffective and potentially harmful psychological interventions for obsessive-compulsive disorder. *OCD Newsletter, 33*(1), 14–19.

Meczekalski, B., Podfigurna-Stopa, A., & Katulski, K. (2013). Long-term consequences of anorexia nervosa. *Maturitas, 75*(3), 215–220.

Melzack, R. (2011). The story of pain. *The Psychologist, 24*(6), 470–471.

Nutt, D. J., & Sharpe, M. (2008). Uncritical positive regard? Issues in the efficacy and safety of psychotherapy. *Psychopharm, 22*(1), 3–6.

Orth, D., Button, C., Davids, K., & Seifert, L. (2017). What current research tells us about skill acquisition in climbing? In L. Seifert, P. Wolf, & A. Schweizer, *The Science of Climbing and Mountaineering* (pp. 196–209). Abingdon: Routledge.

Orth, D., Davids, K., & Seifert, L. (2016). Coordination in climbing: Effect of skill, practice and constraints manipulation. *Sports Medicine, 46*, 255–268.

Orth, D., van der Kamp, J., Memmert, D., & Savelsbergh, G. J. (2017). Creative motor actions as emerging from movement variability. *Frontiers in Psychology, 8*, 1903.

Pageaux, B., & Lepers, R. (2018). The effects of mental fatigue on sport-related performance. In S. Marcora, & M. Sarkar, *Sport and the Brain: The Science of Preparing, Enduring and Winning, Part C.* Amsterdam: Elsevier.

Pain Management. Meditation for Pain Relief. (n.d.). Retrieved from Meditainment: https://www.meditainment.com/pain-management-meditation

Perry, J. (2020). *Performing Under Pressure.* London: Routledge.

Peters, S. (2012). *The Chimp Paradox.* London: Ebury Publishing.

Pincus, D., & Sheikh, A. A. (2009). *Imagery for Pain Relief.* London: Routledge.

Pjipers, J., Oudejans, R. R., Bakker, F. C., & Beek, P. J. (2006). The role of anxiety in perceiving and realizing affordances. *Ecological Psychology, 18*(3), 131–161. doi:10.1207/s15326969eco1803_1

Prochaska, J. O., & DiClemente, C. C. (1983). Stages and processes of self-change of smoking: Toward an integral model of change. *Journal of Consulting and Clinical Psychology, 51*(3), 390–395.

Raue, M., Streicher, B., Lermer, E., & Frey, D. (2019). Perceived safety while engaging in risk sports. *Perceived Safety, 1*, 139–150.

Rubin, D. C. (1986). *Autobiographical Memory.* Cambridge: Cambridge University Press.

Salkovskis, P. (1991). The importance of behaviour in the maintenance of anxiety and panic: A cognitive account. *Behavioural Psychology, 19*(1), 6–19. doi:10.1071/S0141347300011472

Sanchez, X., & Torregrosa, M. (2005). El papel de los factores psicológicos en la escalada deportiva: un análisis cualitativo. *Revista de psicologia del deporte, 14*(2), 177–194.

Sanchez, X., Torregrossa, M., Woodman, T., Jones, G., & Llewellyn, D. (2019). Identification of parameters that predict sport climbing performance. *Frontiers in Psychology, 10*, 1294.

Seifert, L., Cordier, R., Orth, D., Courtine, Y., & Croft, J. L. (2017). Role of route previewing strategies on climbing fluency and exploratory movements. *PLoS ONE, 12*(4). e0176306

Seifert, L., Orth, D., Button, C., & Davids, K. (2017). How expert climbers use perception and action during successful climbing performance. In L. Seifert, P. Wolf, & A. Schweizer, *The Science of Climbing and Mountaineering* (pp. 181–195). Abingdon: Routledge.

Singh, N., Singh, J., Adkins, A., Singh, A. N., & Winton, A. S. (2008). *A Trainer's Manual for Meditation on the Soles of the Feet: A Mindful Method of Anger Management.* Virginia: One Publications.

Slavin, S. (2018). Medical student mental health: Challenges and opportunities. *Medical Science Educator, 28 (Suppl)*, S13–S15.

Smith, D., Wright, C., Allsopp, A., & Westhead, H. (2007). It's all in the mind: PETTLEP-based imagery and sports performance. *Journal of Applied Sport Psychology, 19*(1), 80–92.

Smith, P. (2009). *Climbing Games*. Caernarfon: Pesda Press.

Strosahl, K. D., Wilson, K. G., & Hayes, S. C. (1999). *Acceptance and Commitment Therapy: An Experiential Approach to Behaviour Change*. New York: Guilford Press.

Teixidor-Batlle, C., Ventura, C., & Andres, A. (2021). Eating disorder symptoms in elite Spanish athletes: Prevalence and sport-specific weight pressures. *Frontiers in Psychology, 11*, 3612.

Vanderkam, L. (2018). *Off the Clock: Feel Less Busy While Getting More Done*. Boston: Little, Brown Book Group.

Vealey, R. S., & Chase, M. A. (2008). Self-confidence in sport. In T. S. Horn, *Advances in Sport Psychology* (pp. 68–97, 430–435). Champaign, Illinois: Human Kinetics.

Wenzlaff, R. M., & Wegner, D. M. (2000). Thought suppression. *Annual Review of Psychology, 51*(1), 59–91.

Williams, R. (2021). *Fear of Falling Workbook*. https://smartclimbing.co.uk/product/fear-of-falling-workbook/

Wolpe, J. (1990). *The Practice of Behavior Therapy*. Oxford: Pergamon Press.

Woodman, T., Hardy, L., Barlow, M., & Le Scanff, C. (2010). Motives for participation in prolonged engagement high-risk sports: An agentic emotion regulation perspective. *Psychology of Sport and Exercise, 11*(5), 345–352.

Zaccaro, A., Piarulli, A., Laurino, M., Garbella, E., Menicucci, D., Neri, B., & Gemignali, A. (2018). How breath-control can change your life: A systematic review on psycho-physiological correlates of slow breathing. *Frontiers in Human Neuroscience, 12*, 353.

Zeman, A., Dewar, M., & Della Sala, S. (2015). Lives without imagery - Congenital aphantasia. *Cortex, 73*, 378–380.

Zerubavel, N., & Messman-Moore, T. L. (2013). Staying present: Incorporating mindfulness into therapy for dissociation. *Mindfulness. 6*(2), 303–314.